THE WORLD OF SCIENCE

HOW DOES IT WORK?

THE WORLD OF SCIENCE
HOW DOES IT WORK?

CHRIS COOPER
& JANE INSLEY

Facts On File Publications
New York, New York ● Bicester, England

HOW DOES IT WORK?

Copyright © 1986 by Orbis Publishing Limited,
London

First published in the United States of America in
1986 by Facts on File, Inc., 460 Park Avenue South,
New York, N.Y. 10016

First published in Great Britain in 1986 by
Orbis Publishing Limited, London

**Library of Congress Cataloging in Publication
Data**
Main entry under title:
World of Science

   Includes index.
   Summary: A twenty-five volume encyclopedia of
scientific subjects, designed for eight- to twelve-year-
olds.
One volume is entirely devoted to projects.
   1. Science—Dictionaries, Juvenile.   1. Science—
Dictionaries
Q121.J86   1984   500   84-1654

ISBN: 0-8160-1066-8

Printed in Italy
10 9 8 7 6 5 4 3 2 1

Consultant editors
Eleanor Felder, Former Managing Editor, **New Book
of Knowledge**
James Neujahr, Dean of the School of Education, City
College of New York
Ethan Signer, Professor of Biology, Massachusetts
Institute of Technology
J. Tuzo Wilson, Director General, Ontario Science
Centre

Previous pages
Astronauts on Earth
learning to handle a
lunar landing craft in
preparation for their
descent to the moon.

Editor Penny Clarke
Designer Roger Kohn

CONTENTS

I MANKIND IN MOVEMENT

Airplane **6**
Helicopter **12**
Glider **14**
Hovercraft **15**
Motorcycle **16**
Rocket **18**
Parachute **21**

2 POWER AT COMMAND

Electricity **22**
Engines and motors **28**
Machines **33**
Nuclear energy **36**
Turbine **40**
Explosive **42**
Perpetual motion **44**

3 EXTENDING OUR SENSES

Geiger counter **46**
Microphone **47**
Submarine **50**
Space flight **52**
Robot **60**

Glossary **62**
Index **64**

Note There are some unusual words in this book. They are explained in the Glossary on pages 62–63. The first time each word is used in the text it is printed in *italics*.

►Two competitors in a cross-country motorcycle race duel for the lead.

AIRPLANE

The Boeing 747 jumbo jet is a 350-*tonne* (380-ton) monster that can carry 490 passengers at 800 kph (500 mph), in a non-stop Atlantic crossing. It took less than 80 years to develop this huge airliner from a fragile, kitelike craft that struggled into the air for less than a minute in 1903 to make the world's first powered flight by a heavier-than-air machine.

An *airplane* is an aircraft that is driven by engines and is held up by force generated by air flowing over its wings. (A balloon, on the other hand, floats in the air because it is filled with lighter-than-air gas.) The ancestor of the airplane was the glider (page 14), which has wings but no engine.

The first glider, the size of one of today's model planes, was made by an Englishman, Sir George Cayley, in 1804. He continued his experiments and in 1849, a boy made a flight in a glider towed by Cayley. A few years later a man made a flight in another of Cayley's gliders, without having to be towed.

Cayley knew that his craft needed light, powerful engines to make them into a practical form of transport, but no such engine existed in his day. Occasionally people proposed using steam engines to power airplanes, but they were too heavy and not powerful enough.

In the 1890s two American brothers, Orville and Wilbur Wright, began making experiments with gliders. They realized that the petrol or gasoline engine used in cars could power an aircraft. But there were no suitable engines in existence at that time, so they had to design and build one themselves.

▼Planes are kept up by Bernoulli's principle, which states that air pressure (red arrows) decreases when air flow (white lines) speeds up. Here air flowing through a tube is forced to speed up because the tube becomes narrower. The pressure drops in that part of the tube.

▼A kite is held up by the pressure of the wind (red arrows) pushing on the underside. Bernoulli's principle is not used at all. The wind also creates a backward push, called drag (yellow arrow). The kite's cord overcomes the drag and stops the kite from being blown away.

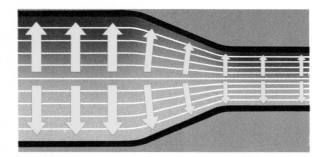

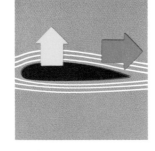

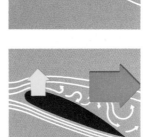

▲A plane's wing is curved more strongly on the upper edge than on the lower. The air has to flow faster above the wing than it does below it, so there is a big difference between the air pressure below and above the wing. This difference is the lift on the wing (red arrow).

▲If a wing's angle is too low, the lift (red arrow) is reduced. The drag (yellow arrow) is also increased. If the wing is at too great an angle (near left), it 'stalls'. The airflow above it is broken up, reducing lift and increasing drag, which could cause the plane to crash.

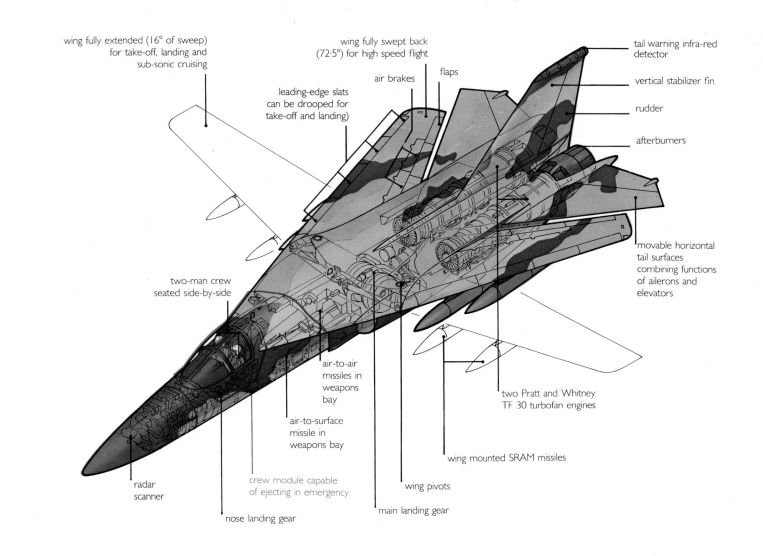

wing fully extended (16° of sweep) for take-off, landing and sub-sonic cruising

wing fully swept back (72·5°) for high speed flight

flaps

air brakes

leading-edge slats can be drooped for take-off and landing)

tail warning infra-red detector

vertical stabilizer fin

rudder

afterburners

two-man crew seated side-by-side

movable horizontal tail surfaces combining functions of ailerons and elevators

air-to-air missiles in weapons bay

air-to-surface missile in weapons bay

two Pratt and Whitney TF 30 turbofan engines

wing mounted SRAM missiles

radar scanner

crew module capable of ejecting in emergency

wing pivots

nose landing gear

main landing gear

The first aircraft flights

After many experiments, the brothers were ready to make their first attempts at manned flight on 17 December 1903. Orville piloted the first flight, lying stretched out on his stomach – the 'aircraft' had no seat. The brothers made four flights that day, the longest being 260 m (852 ft).

The principles on which the Wrights' machine operated are those on which a modern aircraft depends. To counteract the machine's weight, an upward force called lift must be generated by the air flowing over the wings. The wing is cambered – that is, more strongly curved on the upper than on the lower surface. Air flowing over the upper surface has to travel farther, and therefore faster, than air passing beneath the wing. When any fluid, such as air or water, moves faster, its pressure drops. (This is called Bernoulli's principle, after Jacques Bernoulli, a Swiss scientist who lived from 1654 to 1705.) So the air pressure

above a moving airplane wing is lower than the pressure below it. The difference in pressure provides lift to keep the airplane up.

The Wrights' airplane was a biplane – that is, it had two main sets of wings, one mounted above the other. The large wing area provided a large amount of lift. Since the 1930s, however, most new aircraft have been designed as monoplanes, which have one set of main wings.

Guiding aircraft

The Wrights made their plane turn by pulling wires that reduced the camber of one wing, so that it lost some of its lift. Then that wing would drop and the plane would turn in that direction. But a better way of providing control was soon developed. On each wing there is an aileron – a hinged section at the rear of the wing. If the aileron is lowered, the wing appears to be more curved or, to put it another way, the camber of the wing is increased. The lift over that wing

▲The F-111 variable-geometry fighter-bomber, built by the American General Dynamics Corporation. With its wings forward it can take off with large loads from runways of moderate length. With wings swept back it can fly at twice the speed of sound.

7

▲In level flight at constant speed, the lift created by the wings (a) counteracts the weight of the plane (b). The thrust of the engines (c) overcomes the drag of the air on the plane (d).

►A plane rolls using the ailerons on its main wings (top). It climbs and dives using the elevators on its tailplane (middle) and turns left or right using its rudder.

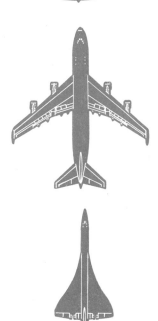

►Airplanes grew more streamlined as their speeds increased. Swept wings appeared, and then the delta wings of supersonic aircraft.

▲'Spirit of St Louis', piloted by Charles A. Lindbergh, was the first airplane to cross the Atlantic non-stop.

It made the crossing from west to east in 1927, taking 33½ hours. Today *Concorde* takes a little under 3½ hours.

▲A British Sopwith Pup fighter of World War 1. It was little more than 10 years since the Wright brothers' first primitive plane, yet the development of aircraft had made huge strides.

The Pup was a biplane, with two sets of main wings for greater lift. It was controlled by moving 'control surfaces' – hinged sections of the wings, tailplane and tail fin.

▼Spitfire fighters played an important part in World War 2 in beating off the attacks of the German *Luftwaffe*. These British-built Spitfires are being prepared for delivery to Russia.

increases, and the wing rises. At the same time, the aileron on the other wing is raised slightly, reducing the camber. The lift decreases on that wing, and the wing drops. If the plane is tilted to, say, the right, the lift generated by its wings will pull it to the right.

When turning the pilot uses the plane's rudder as well as the ailerons. The rudder is a hinged section on the upright tail fin. If the rudder is swung to the right, into the stream of air rushing past the plane, the tail is forced to the left, turning the nose to the right.

At the aircraft's tail there is a pair of small wings, called the tailplane. These have hinged sections, called elevators. If both the elevators are raised, the tailplane's lift is reduced, the tail drops and the plane climbs. If the elevators are lowered, the tail rises and the plane goes into a dive.

The pilot controls the ailerons and elevators by means of the 'joystick'. It looks a little like a car's steering wheel, but it can be pulled backwards and pushed forwards, as well as turned. On small aircraft there are also pedals to control the rudder. And next to the pilot's seat there are levers that control the flow of fuel to the engines and therefore the *power* that they generate.

The coming of jets

All planes until World War 2 were propeller-driven. As the propellers spun, they threw a stream of air backwards. This created a '*reaction*' force that pushed the plane forward. In the same way, a ship is pushed forward as its propeller forces water backwards. In the 1930s, however, engineers in Britain and Germany developed the jet engine. This sucked air in through an intake at the front, compressed it, warmed it by burning fuel, and threw it out at a much higher velocity (speed). The backward motion of the hot gas formed by this process produced a reaction that pushed the engine forward. This is also used for propelling rockets (page 18). The first jet-engined aircraft to fly was the German Heinkel He 178, on 27 August 1939. Jet-engined fighters were built by the British and Germans in 1944. After World War 2 faster and faster jet planes were built, capable of reaching speeds far beyond those of the fastest propeller-driven aircraft. Soon jet fighters were travelling faster than sound, or more than 1200 kph (760 mph) at sea level. Jet airliners took over from propeller-driven airliners, too. Aircraft were designed with sweptback wings, since these reduced problems of handling the planes at high speeds.

▲ A Hawker Siddeley Harrier of the US Marine Corps. This 'jump-jet' can take off vertically. The nozzles of its Pegasus jet engine swivel to give downward thrust when taking off or landing. In flight they swivel to point rearwards. The Harrier is flown from aircraft carriers and from small battlefield airstrips where a long takeoff run is impossible.

◀ One of the earliest jet fighters, the swept-wing F-47 Saber.

▼ The thin wings of a B-52 jet bomber bend upwards as it cruises. The B-52 has eight powerful engines housed in pods slung under its wings, and it has an intercontinental range.

Sonic booms

When an aircraft is travelling at less than the speed of sound, the noise of its flight travels ahead of it and disturbs the air. This makes it easier for the air to 'get out of the way' of the plane. When a plane is travelling faster than sound, the air has no 'warning'. Extra thrust is needed to force the aircraft through the air. And a 'shock wave', or pressure wave, spreads out from the plane. The shock wave is shaped like a cone, trailing behind the plane. The plane is at the cone's point. The wave touches the ground beneath the aircraft, some distance behind it. There is a momentary increase in *pressure* as the shock wave passes, and people on the ground hear a bang, called a sonic boom. ('Sonic' means 'to do with sound'.) Sonic booms are not only loud but can also be dangerous – they can break windows and shake buildings if the aircraft flies below an altitude of about 10,000 m (30,000 ft).

Supersonic flight

Jet airliners took over from propeller-driven airliners during the 1960s. But the first supersonic airliner did not come into service until 1976. This is the *Concorde*, built jointly by the British and the French. It can cruise at speeds of over 1,500 kph (1,000 mph) on its trans-Atlantic crossings. It has a triangular wing – called a delta wing, because delta, the fourth letter of the Greek alphabet, is triangular. When Concorde passes the speed of sound, and shock waves build up around it, fuel has to be pumped from the front of the plane to the back to prevent the nose from dipping suddenly. And when the plane lands, it has to do so in a tilted-up position. As a result the nose of the aircraft has to be made to 'droop' during landing to give the pilot a view of the runway.

It is impossible to design a wing shape that is very efficient at all speeds, from low landing speeds to high supersonic ones. So some planes are designed to change their wing shapes in flight. The American F-111 fighter-bomber is one of these swing-wing or 'variable-geometry' aircraft. For takeoff and landing, its wings are in the fully forward position, with very little sweepback. In the air they can be swung back until, with the tailplane, they form a delta shape for supersonic speeds.

A new type of engine

Progress in jet engines has revolutionized airliner transport. The turbofan is powerful, yet relatively quiet, and it is economical of fuel. Without it there would be no jumbo jets. And it is these aircraft, which are powered by turbofans and can carry huge numbers of passengers, that have made air travel cheaper than ever before.

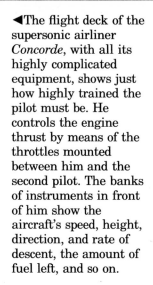

◀The flight deck of the supersonic airliner *Concorde*, with all its highly complicated equipment, shows just how highly trained the pilot must be. He controls the engine thrust by means of the throttles mounted between him and the second pilot. The banks of instruments in front of him show the aircraft's speed, height, direction, and rate of descent, the amount of fuel left, and so on.

▲A Boeing 747, one of the largest and most successful of modern jet airliners.

▼The supersonic airliner *Concorde* coming in to land. It travels at twice the speed of sound over the Atlantic, where its sonic boom will disturb no one. Its nose is 'dropped' during landing to let the pilot see the runway.

HELICOPTER

▼A passenger-carrying helicopter. The main rotors turn counter-clockwise, and the helicopter tends to rotate in the opposite direction. The tail rotor pushes to the right to prevent this. The angle at which the rotors cut through the air is called their pitch. The pilot changes the pitch of all rotors at once, using the collective pitch stick, to increase or decrease the lift. Increasing the pitch of each rotor while it is toward the rear of the machine, using the cyclic pitch stick, increases the lift at the back and tilts the helicopter forward (centre right), so that it moves forward. Backward and sideways movements can be carried out in a similar way.

The helicopter is a marvellously agile aircraft, able to take off and land on tiny patches of level ground and to fly backwards and sideways as easily as forwards. Though it flies more slowly and carries smaller loads than an airplane, there are many tasks that only the helicopter can perform.

The first helicopters
Some of the earliest pioneers of flight tried to build machines that would take off and land vertically. In 1907, two Frenchmen, working independently, succeeded. Louis Breguet's machine had four rotors, each on the end of a long arm. Helpers standing on the ground had to steady the machine during its one-minute 'flight'. The machine was powered by a

petrol engine, as was Paul Cornu's rival helicopter. Cornu's machine stayed up for less than 30 seconds.

Modern helicopters
The Wright brothers had made the world's first flight in a powered airplane four years earlier (page 7). The rapid development of airplanes after that overshadowed the clumsy helicopter. In fact it was over 30 years before the helicopter as we know it made its appearance. This was a helicopter, with powered rotors, built by a German, Heinrich Focke, in 1936. Called the Fa-61, it had twin rotors turning in opposite directions. When a helicopter has a single rotor, its body tends to turn in the opposite direction to the rotor. Having

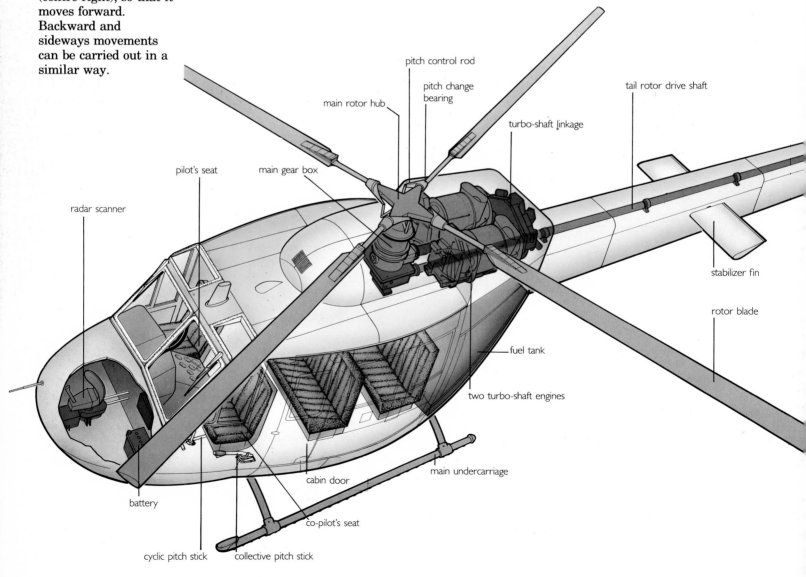

pitch control rod

pitch change bearing

main rotor hub

tail rotor drive shaft

turbo-shaft linkage

pilot's seat

main gear box

radar scanner

stabilizer fin

rotor blade

fuel tank

two turbo-shaft engines

main undercarriage

cabin door

battery

co-pilot's seat

cyclic pitch stick

collective pitch stick

wo rotors turning in opposite directions
olves this problem. The Fa-61 reached a
peed of 120 kph (75 mph), and an
ltitude of over 3 km (2 miles). It was
ollowed by the Fa-223, a much larger
machine that could carry six passengers.

The first successful single-rotor
helicopter was built in the United States
n 1939, by the Russian-born Igor
ikorsky. Modern helicopters follow his
lesign.

Rotors and lift

Each blade of the main rotor is shaped
like an airplane's wing to create lift as it
moves through the air. The pilot can
hange the 'pitch' of the blades to vary
he amount of lift. Imagine that a ruler
ying on a table represents a rotor blade.
f you lift one side of the ruler while the
ther stays flat on the table, you are

mitating the movement of the blade
when its pitch – the angle at which it
meets the air – is increased. Increasing
he pitch of all the blades at once
ncreases the lift, and the helicopter rises.
Decreasing the pitch causes the helicopter
o descend. Increasing the pitch of each
blade only in the rearward part of its
motion causes an increased lift at the
rear. This makes the helicopter tilt
orward, and then the rotor blades' lift
pulls it forward. To make the helicopter
go to the left, the pitch of each blade must
be increased as it passes round the right-
hand part of its circle, and so on.

The helicopter was scarcely used during
World War 2, but has proved its military
value since. It can carry troops and their
supplies into jungle clearings where no
plane could land. It has countless peaceful
uses, too. It can rescue stranded climbers,

◄This helicopter is
hovering while it
lowers goods on to the
deck of a ship in the
Arctic ocean. The
rotors are blurred by
the speed at which
they are turning. Each
one is a moving wing,
creating 'lift' that
supports the helicopter.

the crews of sinking ships and people
trapped on the tops of burning buildings.
It can ferry food and medical supplies into
areas devastated by floods or earthquakes.
It can carry passengers from city centres
to airports, and it is the fastest way of
transporting workers and supplies
between the mainland and offshore oil
drilling rigs.

Autogyros

Although helicopters were developed later
than airplanes, a near relative of the
modern helicopter was successfully
developed in the 1920s and 1930s. This
was the autogyro. It was an airplane with
wings and a propeller at the front, but
with a rotor mounted on top of it. The
rotor was not connected to the engine;
instead, the flow of air past the aircraft
made the rotor turn. (The word 'autogyro'
means 'self-turning'.) As it turned, the
rotor provided extra 'lift', so that the
engine did not need to be so powerful and
could use less fuel. If the engine failed,
the autogyro did not crash – it just glided
gently to the ground, helped by the lift
provided by the rotor.

The autogyro's Spanish inventor, Juan
de la Cierva, flew an autogyro across the
English Channel in 1928 to demonstrate
that it was a practical machine. Hundreds
of autogyros were made during the 1930s,
but as helicopters developed and improved
the market for autogyros disappeared.

GLIDER

▲American military gliders and transport planes lined up for take off at the start of the Allied invasion of Germany, March 1945.

▼Hang gliders were first used by pioneers of flying to find out more about air currents and their effect on the wings of aircraft. They are actually large man-carrying kites.

A glider, or sailplane, is an unpowered winged aircraft. In fact a glider is just like an ordinary airplane except that it has no engine and is very light. When a sailplane takes off, it has to 'borrow' power. It is towed along fast by a rope that is pulled by a winch, a car or a powered airplane. When the glider is travelling fast enough, the air flowing over its curved wing surfaces creates 'lift', which makes the glider rise off the ground (page 6).

Once airborne, a glider will start to descend because it has no engine to help it remain in the air. But a glider is designed to be very light in weight. Its large wings cushion its descent and also generate lift. So the glider comes down at a very shallow angle. And if the pilot can find a current of rising air, the glider will be lifted upwards.

These currents of rising air are called 'thermals'. The word 'thermal' means 'to do with heat'. The air rises when it is warmer than the air surrounding it. A ploughed field is likely to be warmer than the ground around it, and so a glider pilot would hope to find a thermal above it. There are often thermals over the coast, because the land is usually warmer than the sea during the day.

Today, gliders are almost entirely used for recreation and leisure – they are cheaper to buy and fly than powered aircraft. There is much competition among glider pilots to set records for time in the air, distance flown and so on. Using thermals, the glider pilot can soar to great heights. On record-breaking flights, gliders have climbed to altitudes of over 13 km (8 miles).

Hang gliders

Another type of glider is the hang glider. It is a large triangular kite, and beneath it is a frame from which the pilot hangs. To launch the hang glider the pilot jumps from a cliff or some other high ground. The pilot steers by shifting his weight right or left.

►Gliders can only stay airborne if the pilot can find thermals with which to gain altitude, between periods when the glider is descending.

HOVERCRAFT

The hovercraft is not a ship, an airplane, or a car. It 'flies' over land or water, just above the surface, supported on a cushion of high-pressure air. Another name for it is 'air cushion vehicle'.

One or several powerful fans are built into the hovercraft. These suck in air from above the craft and pump it out at the bottom. The air cannot easily escape from underneath, so pressure builds up and lifts the craft up. Propellers or jet engines drive the hovercraft forwards, sideways or backwards. There is very little friction between the air cushion and the water or ground beneath, so the hovercraft can travel fast without using too much fuel.

Huge hovercraft are used as ferries across the English Channel. Each one can carry hundreds of passengers and dozens of cars and buses between England and France, far faster than ships can. These sea-going hovercraft have flexible rubber 'skirts' to help trap the air beneath them.

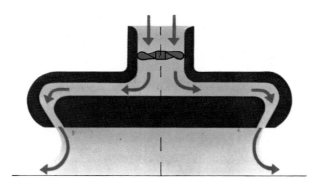

This results in higher pressure and helps to keep the craft we above the water, undisturbed by high waves.

Hovercraft are used for military patrols in coastal and swampy areas, because of their ability to travel on land and sea. In factories, heavy loads can be carried on 'hover-pallets' – platforms supported on cushions of air. The air supply comes from a fixed air pump connected to the pallet by an air hose. There are even 'hover lawnmowers', which have no wheels and are easy to move over the grass.

◄Diagram showing how a hovercraft works. Air is sucked in at the top by a fan and blown out beneath the craft. In this type, the air is blown inwards to form a 'wall' that traps the air cushion. In other types, a rubber 'skirt' is used instead.

▼A giant hovercraft used as a car ferry across the English Channel. Gas turbine engines drive the propellers and four fans.

MOTORCYCLE

▲Motorcycle racing is now an important international sport, with large prizes at stake. Cornering at speed, this competitor leans well towards the centre of the track. But if he misjudges the angle and leans too far, the bike may skid.

The first motorcycles were built in the 1860s – but they were very different from the sleek, powerful roadsters of today. They were driven by steam engines fuelled with charcoal or alcohol and they moved slowly and jerkily. But soon steam tricycles were being built in hundreds in Philadelphia, in the United States.

Then the newly invented petrol (gasoline) engine was harnessed to power motorcycles. The first practical machines were built in the 1890s. In Paris, two brothers, Michael and Eugene Werner, built a motorcycle in which the engine was fixed on top of the handlebars and drove the front wheels. But by 1901 they had adopted the layout that all modern motorcycles have. The engine was slung low down between the wheels and drove the rear wheel. It was controlled by twisting the handlebar grips.

At the same time as the Werners were building their first machines, two German engineers, Hildebrand and Wolfmuller, built their motorcycles with petrol (gasoline) engines. These vehicles had a throttle control on the handlebars and a dropped frame so that they could be ridden by women as well as men.

The French De Dion tricycle of 1895 had a petrol (gasoline) engine mounted behind the rear axle of a pedal tricycle. The enormous popularity of the machine helped to establish the motorcycle industry.

Engines with pistons

In a petrol or gasoline engine, the fuel is burnt inside metal cylinders. The expanding gases push pistons (page 30), which in turn drive the wheels. Motorcycles may have one, two, three or four pistons, and they may drive the rear wheel by means of a connecting chain or a spinning shaft called a driveshaft. The engine cylinders may be positioned vertically, horizontally or at an angle. They can be recognized by their cooling vanes – flat metal plates that have a large surface area, and so help get rid of the cylinders' heat to the air.

Some motorcycle engines are of the 'two-stroke' type. Each time some fuel is exploded in the cylinder (by an electric spark), the piston travels once down the cylinder and once back. More powerful engines are of the 'four-stroke' type, similar to car engines. In these engines the piston makes two downward and two upward movements after each spark (page 30).

The purpose of gears

Motorcycles have *gears* just as cars do. Gears are a series of cogged wheels that convert the speed of the driveshaft or drive chain to the speed of the wheels, because frequently they do not run at the same speed. Sometimes, for example, the engine has to run very fast to deliver a lot of power, while the wheels are still turning relatively slowly. This is the case when the motorcycle is climbing a hill or accelerating from a low speed. When cruising at a high speed on a level road, the engine may need to run more slowly – yet the wheels will be turning much faster.

To change gear, the driver has to disconnect the engine from the wheels. This is usually done by twisting the clutch control on one of the handlebars, although sometimes gears are changed by means of a pedal. But the arrangement of controls differs from machine to machine. The throttle, which allows more petrol (gasoline) to reach the engine, so that it puts out more power, is also usually controlled by a handlebar twist-grip.

Many motorcycles on the roads can go much faster than 145 kph (90 mph) – though in most countries this is legal only on special race tracks. A world motorcycle speed record was achieved in 1978 by a Japanese-built Kawasaki machine. It travelled at 513 kph (319 mph). However, it had three wheels – not two.

▲Motorcycles have shock absorbers to protect the rider and the engine from the jolts and vibration that the wheels receive on even the smoothest roads. The coiled spring of the rear-wheel shock absorber can be seen here. On this motorcycle the rear wheel is turned not by a chain but by a driveshaft, which you can see connecting the wheel hub to the engine.

◄A motorcycle and sidecar combination take a bend on a race track. The passenger leans out, skimming the ground, to counteract the force that tends to turn the machine over. Streamlined shells over the cycle and sidecar reduce wind resistance.

►The snow scooter is an unusual adaptation of the motorcycle. It is fitted with skis so that it can travel across the snowfields of.

ROCKET

▲*Columbia*, the first of the space orbiters, stands on the launch- pad ready for its first take off, 12 April, 1981.

The most powerful motor known to human beings is the rocket. It is the only one that can propel spacecraft to other planets and put satellites into orbit around the Earth. Yet it is one of the easiest to understand, for even the giant space shuttle works on the same principles as the rockets you see at firework displays.

The toy firework was probably invented in China over 700 years ago. It has changed little since then. It is simply a tube filled with gunpowder packed very tightly. When the flame from the rocket's burning fuse reaches the gunpowder, there is a violent chemical reaction. Different substances in the gunpowder combine and turn into hot gases at high pressure. They try to expand, and if the tube were closed at both ends, the gases would tear it apart. But there is an opening at the lower end of the tube, and the gases rush out, forming a bright glowing trail, called the 'exhaust'.

It is the force generated by the chemical reaction that pushes out the exhaust gases. But whenever a force is exerted on something, there is a 'reaction' – an equally strong force in the opposite direction. For example, when you fire a rifle, you feel it 'kick' against your shoulder. The gun is pushed back by the reaction to the force that drives the bullet forward. If you were standing on roller skates while carrying a heavy bag, and you were unwise enough to throw the bag away from you, you would find yourself rolling away in the opposite direction. The reaction to your throwing the bag would have given you an equal and opposite push. In the same way, the explosion of the gunpowder in the rocket tube not only pushes out the exhaust gases but generates a reaction force that drives the rocket in the opposite direction. (Jet engines, page 9, work on the same principle.)

Fuel for rockets

The firework rocket is an example of a 'solid-fuel' rocket. Some very large modern rockets also use solid fuels – for example, two solid-fuel booster rockets

►Three unmanned rockets take off together to collect information about the upper atmosphere. The automatic instruments on these Javelin rockets will radio the information they collect back to Earth.

carry the space shuttle 45 km (28 miles) high before its main motor takes over. But rockets using liquid fuels are much more powerful and easier to control, and these are used for travel in space.

Liquid rocket fuel actually consists of two different liquids, which combine when they are mixed. One is called the *propellant*. The other is called the *oxidant*, because it provides oxygen that combines with the propellant. (In a solid-fuel rocket the propellant and oxidant are different solids, mixed together.) The chemical process in a rocket is simply burning, and whenever anything burns it combines with oxygen. Often the oxidant consists of pure liquid oxygen, which has to be kept very cold, because oxygen boils at −183°C (−297°F).

The oxidant and propellant are stored in separate fuel tanks. When the rocket is to fire, motors begin to pump the two liquids into the combustion (burning) chamber, where they combine and turn into hot gas. (A spark or a hot wire may be used to start the fuel burning.) The combustion process can be stopped at any time by cutting off the supply of fuel.

The Saturn V rockets

The largest rockets ever launched were the Saturn V rockets that blasted American astronauts to the Moon. Each stood 119 m (363 ft) high, and actually consisted of several 'stages', each one a separate rocket. The first stage contained five engines, each with its own combustion chamber and exhaust nozzle, burning paraffin and liquid oxygen. This stage developed 3500 tonnes (3860 tons) of thrust. When its fuel was used up, this stage fell away so that there was less weight for the second-stage engines to lift. The second stage also contained five engines, burning liquid hydrogen and liquid oxygen. When the second stage fell away, the third stage, a single engine also burning liquid hydrogen and liquid oxygen, took over. There were further rockets on the lunar module, which

▼These rockets are shown to the same scale. The figures underneath show how much thrust their engines could produce. The Bumper was an early American rocket adapted from the German V-2 rocket bomb. It was unmanned and could not go into orbit. The others all carried men into space.

Bumper	Mercury Atlas	Vostok	Gemini Titan III C	Apollo Saturn V
30,480 kg	163,300 kg	499,000 kg	1,381,600 kg	3,451,900 kg

180 cm

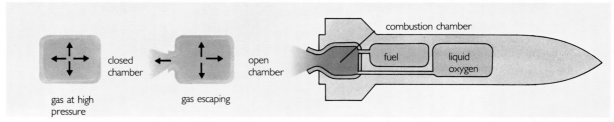

closed chamber

gas at high pressure

open chamber

gas escaping

combustion chamber

fuel

liquid oxygen

►If rocket fuel were burned in a closed chamber, the hot gases produced would press on all walls equally and so the chamber would not move. But if the gas can escape from one end of the chamber, there is an unbalanced force on the opposite wall, which will push the chamber in that direction. This is the principle of the rocket. In large rockets the fuel is a liquid and is burned by mixing it with liquid oxygen in the combustion chamber.

travelled on towards the Moon. The lunar module weighed only 50 tonnes (55 tons), compared with the 2,900 tonnes (3,200 tons) of the Saturn V that had launched it.

Rockets can work in the *vacuum* of space because they take their own oxygen along with them to enable their fuel to burn. Jet engines could not work in space because they use oxygen from the air that they draw in – and there is no air in

space. Apart from this, the principle of the jet is very similar to that of the rocket.

In the distant future long space journeys may be made using nuclear-powered rockets. These would use nuclear reactors to heat gases that would expand and provide thrust. The thrust would be relatively weak, but could be kept up for the months or even years that would be needed for a flight to the outermost planets.

◄The American orbiter Challenger was the first space craft that could be flown back to Earth and be re-used. Two solid-fuel booster rockets carried the orbiter on the first part of its flight. Then the orbiter's own engines took over, using liquid hydrogen from its huge belly tank. This tank is dropped when empty. When the craft returns from orbit, it glides down through the atmosphere and lands on a runway like an airplane.

PARACHUTE

Parachutists can leap from aircraft high above the earth, knowing they will land in perfect safety a few minutes later. Heavy equipment can be pushed out of planes and brought to the ground, dangling beneath a cluster of parachutes, without damage. The resistance of the air cushions the fall – parachutes would be useless on the Moon, where there is no air.

A parachute is made of very light material, such as nylon, and has a very large area, so that it cannot move through the air fast once it has opened. It is connected by dozens of lines to the harness that the parachutist wears.

There are different ways in which a parachute may be opened. Generally the parachutist pulls the ripcord – a cord that releases a small parachute called a 'drogue'. Pulled by the rush of air, the small parachute drags the main parachute out of its pack. Immediately, the speed of the descending parachutist slows down, allowing skilled 'chutists to control very precisely where they land.

Another method of opening the parachute is to have the ripcord connected to a point in the aircraft, so that it is automatically pulled as the parachutist leaves the plane. This method is used in training.

When an airman fires himself from a crashing plane using his ejection seat, he does not have to open his parachute himself. The parachute will open automatically when he has fallen to an altitude where there is enough oxygen to breathe – even if the airman is unconscious during his fall.

Parachutes are used not only to bring people and objects slowly down to the ground but also to slow down fast-moving racing cars, and planes when they land.

▶A free fall parachutist, photographed by a companion as they fell through the sky. They will wait until they are about 600 m (1,800 ft) up before opening their parachutes. An emergency parachute is strapped to the sky diver's chest – for use if the main parachute doesn't open.

▼Sports parachutists compete to see how accurately they can guide themselves to a target on the ground. The slots cut into this parachute help the parachutist to do this. The small 'drogue' parachute that pulls the main parachute out of its pack is visible here just to the right of the main one.

▲Lightning is a natural display of immense electrical power. Electric charges build up in the lower and upper regions of storm clouds. Opposite kinds of charge (positive and negative) are strongly attracted towards each other. Finally this electrical force, or voltage, becomes so great that a current forces its way through the air, either from one part of the cloud to another or between the cloud and the ground. The sudden expansion of the air caused by the heat of the lightning stroke causes the sound of thunder.

ELECTRICITY

It is no exaggeration to say that the modern world runs on electricity. It lights and heats our homes, it powers trains and factory machinery, and it is essential to radio, television, sound recording, computers and hosts of other aspects of our lives. But what is electricity?

Atoms and electrons
Everything is made up of tiny particles called *atoms*. The outermost part of every

atom consists of still smaller particles called *electrons*, whirling around the atom's *nucleus* or central core, just as planets move around the Sun.

Electrons are said to have a 'negative electric charge'. There is also a positive electric charge, which is carried by the atom's nucleus. Positive and negative charges attract each other – in fact, the positive charge of the nucleus normally holds the electrons to the atom. But negative charges repel each other – they try to push each other away. And positive charges also repel other positive charges.

Sometimes electrons escape from their atoms. This happens very easily in some materials, including most metals. Such materials are called electrical conductors. A stream of electrons, called an electric current, can easily flow through a conductor. All electrical devices use electric currents.

▼A huge turbine in an electricity generating plant. Steam produced by coal, oil or nuclear power makes the turbine spin. This in turn makes an electrical generator rotate, producing electricity at high voltage. This turbine could produce enough power to light more than a million homes.

▶Cables slung from tall pylons carry electricity at high voltage from power stations to homes and factories. At sub-stations like this one, the voltage is reduced to a safer level before the electricity is passed on to the consumer.

►The effects of an electric current show how much current is flowing. When the current passes through a light bulb, it creates light and heat. Its magnetic field deflects a compass needle (that is, moves it from its normal position). If the current is increased, the bulb becomes brighter and hotter, and the compass needle is more strongly deflected.

►Voltage is the 'push' that drives a current. Batteries supply voltage, generated by chemical reactions. If a bulb is connected across the terminals of a battery, it will light up and grow hot, showing that current is flowing. If it is connected across two batteries connected together, it will become brighter and hotter, showing that more voltage means more current.

►The resistance of a part of an electrical circuit is the difficulty with which current flows through it. A resistor is a component deliberately included in a circuit to limit the amount of current. If two identical resistors are connected 'in series' with each other (so that the current goes through each in turn), there will be less current than if only one resistor were used.

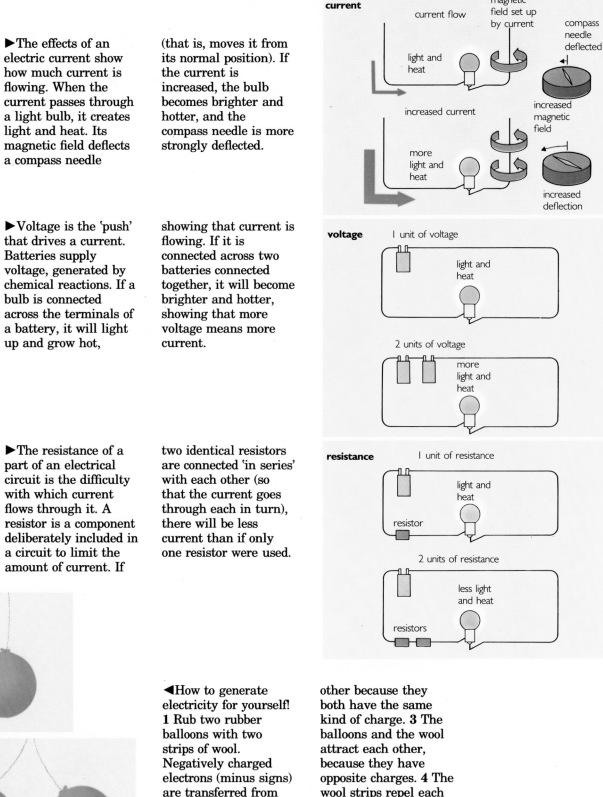

current

current flow

magnetic field set up by current

light and heat

compass needle deflected

increased current

more light and heat

increased magnetic field

increased deflection

voltage   1 unit of voltage

light and heat

2 units of voltage

more light and heat

resistance   1 unit of resistance

light and heat

resistor

2 units of resistance

less light and heat

resistors

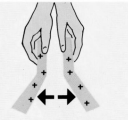

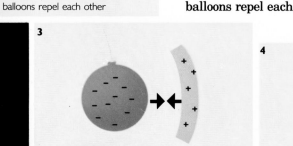

wool

rubbing balloons with wool

balloons repel each other

charged wool and balloon attract each other

wool strips repel each other

◄How to generate electricity for yourself! 1 Rub two rubber balloons with two strips of wool. Negatively charged electrons (minus signs) are transferred from the wool to the balloons. Fixed positive charges (plus signs) are left behind. 2 The balloons repel each other because they both have the same kind of charge. 3 The balloons and the wool attract each other, because they have opposite charges. 4 The wool strips repel each other because they have the same kind of charge – in this case, positive.

How batteries work

When you switch on a pocket torch or flashlight, huge numbers of electrons flow through a thin wire, called a filament, in the bulb. The electrons bump against the atoms of the wire and create heat. The filament glows white-hot. The 'push' that makes the electrons move is called 'voltage'. It is produced by the torch battery. The battery has a metal case containing a chemical paste. In the centre there is a carbon rod. Chemical reactions produce a voltage between the case and the rod. Metal contacts connect one end of the filament to the case and the other to the carbon rod. This forms a 'circuit' – a conducting pathway round which electrons can flow, from the metal case, through the filament to the carbon rod, and back out through the chemical paste to the case. Closing the switch merely closes a gap in the circuit – current cannot flow until the circuit is complete.

Batteries are used to provide the small amounts of power needed in small devices such as portable radios and heart pacemakers. Larger ones are used in cars to 'turn over' the engine to make it start and to operate the lights, indicators and so on. Ordinary batteries become weaker after a while. But some types are 'rechargeable' – if current is forced through them in the reverse direction, the battery becomes usable again. Car batteries are rechargeable. When the engine is running, it turns an electrical generator, which sends current into the battery to 'charge it up'. What happens, put simply, is that coils of wire in the generator are made to turn in a magnetic field (page 27). This movement produces a current.

Electricity for homes and factories

Most of the electrical equipment in homes, shops and factories is powered by electricity that comes not from batteries but from electricity produced in generating stations. This is sent all over the country along the cables that you can see slung from 'pylons', or towers made of metal girders.

Generating stations do not produce electricity by chemical means, as batteries do. Steam is forced through machines

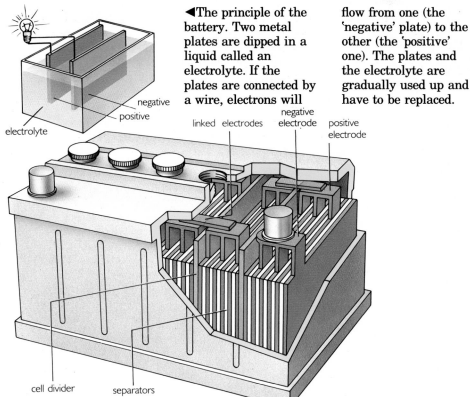

◀The principle of the battery. Two metal plates are dipped in a liquid called an electrolyte. If the plates are connected by a wire, electrons will flow from one (the 'negative' plate) to the other (the 'positive' one). The plates and the electrolyte are gradually used up and have to be replaced.

negative
positive
electrolyte
linked electrodes
negative electrode
positive electrode
cell divider
separators

▲A car battery. It consists of four identical parts, called 'cells'. Each electrode consists of several plates joined together. The negative electrode of each cell is joined to the positive electrode of the next so that the voltages of the cells are added together. This kind of battery is kept 'charged up' by the car's electrical generator, which forces current into it in the reverse direction.

called turbines. These have blades that act like windmill sails, so that the steam makes the turbine spin (page 40). The turbine in turn operates an electrical generator. This is a much larger version of the generator in a car.

Electricity generating stations produce huge voltages. The electricity in overhead power cables is being 'pushed' by as much as 400,000 volts. But this would be far too dangerous for use in homes or even in most factories. So the voltage is 'stepped down', or reduced, at 'sub-stations' before the electricity is supplied to users. The electrical outlets in a British home supply electricity at 240 volts. But there is no standard level. In many European countries home voltage is 120 volts and in the USA it is 110–115 volts.

The steam that turns the turbines in power stations is produced by heating water. The heat may come from burning coal or oil, or from nuclear power (see page 36). In a diesel-electric locomotive, a

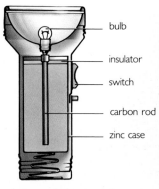

bulb
insulator
switch
carbon rod
zinc case

▲A torch battery is called a dry cell. It is not truly dry, but contains a damp paste in an outer zinc case, which is one electrode. The other electrode is a carbon rod in the centre of the battery. When the switch is closed, current flows round the circuit, through the wire, or filament, in the bulb. The filament glows white-hot.

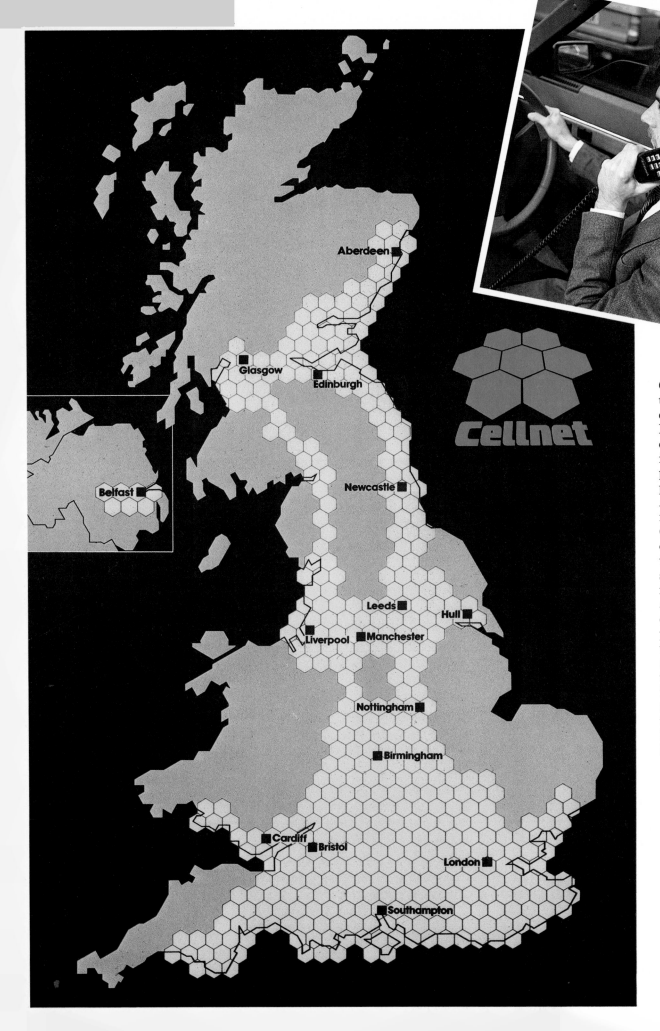

Conventional telephones are connected by cables. Phones in cars cannot, of course, be connected in this way. Cellnet car phones use very low-powered radio signals. A country is divided into areas or cells (**map**), each with its own transmitter, each transmitter using a slightly different radio frequency. Even if you are in the middle of a call (**inset**) when passing from one cell to another, the system automatically transfers to the new frequency in a fraction of a second. Car phones like this are used in the USA, Scandinavia and Britain.

Aberdeen

Glasgow
Edinburgh

Belfast

Newcastle

Leeds
Hull

Liverpool
Manchester

Nottingham

Birmingham

Cardiff
Bristol

London

Southampton

Cellnet

diesel engine drives a generator that produces the electricity that moves the locomotive. Windmills can also drive electrical generators.

Electric motors

Electric motors act in the opposite way to electrical generators. They use an electric current to produce a rotational motion. They depend on the fact that if a wire carrying an electric current is placed in a magnetic field, a force is produced on the wire. In an electric motor, the current flows through coils of wire. The wires are in a magnetic field, and they experience a force that makes them turn. Electric motors are used in food mixers, drills, factory equipment and electric locomotives.

The magnetic field in an electric motor and some other electrical devices may be produced by a magnetic material, like the toy magnets you can buy. But it is more often created by electric current. Every electric current has magnetic effects. If you place a magnetic compass on a table and put an electrical wire near it, you will see a sudden movement of the compass needle when you turn the current on and off. The needle reacts to the magnetic field that appears and disappears as the current flows and then stops. Electricity and magnetism are so closely linked that scientists regard them as two aspects of one thing – electromagnetism.

Electricity and information

Apart from the work that electricity can do in producing light, heat and movement, it is also vital in storing and sending 'information'. An LP contains recorded information about the music on it. Radio waves carry information about the speech or music in the radio programme. When you have a telephone conversation you are sending and receiving information. And electricity is involved in all these things.

Sound consists of vibrations of the air, varying in strength and frequency (frequency is the number of vibrations per second). A microphone converts the sounds that reach it into a rapidly varying electric current which fluctuates

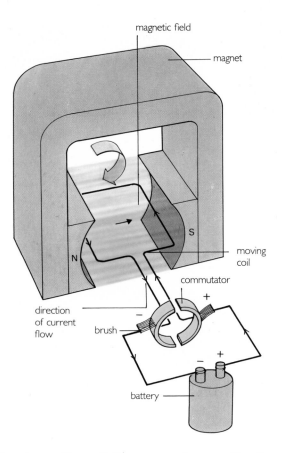

in strength and frequency in exactly the same way as the sounds it receives (page 47). An electrical 'signal' can be sent across continents along telephone wires. Or it can be used to create similar fluctuations in radio waves, for radio waves are generated when electric currents flow back and forth at high frequency. So the information contained in, say, a politician's speech can be flashed around the world in a fraction of a second.

Computers also store, transmit and process information in the form of tiny electrical charges. The electrical circuits in a computer store complicated patterns of electric charge – in the same way that a page of a book contains complicated 'patterns' of letters and numerals. Like the symbols on the page, the electric charges in the computer can represent words and numbers, facts, instructions and calculations. A book can only store information, but a computer can work with it – carrying out calculations, changing the information and exchanging information with the computer operator. Although computers can carry out many hundreds of calculations in a very short time, in fact they use very little electricity.

◄This diagram shows the principle of the electric motor. An electric current is sent through a coil of wire in a magnetic field. The right-hand part of the coil (current flowing into the field) experiences a downward force. The left-hand part experiences an upward force. So the coil rotates in the direction shown. Current is fed to the coil through the commutator and the 'brushes' shown. At each half-turn, the current through the coil is reversed by this arrangement. So, as the part of the coil now at the right passes to the left-hand side, the force on it will switch from being downward to being upward. This makes the coil turn continuously in one direction. Real electric motors are much more complicated than this although this is the basic principle behind them all.

ENGINES AND MOTORS

▶This steam engine was built in 1890 to drive factory machinery. The piston moves back and forth in the horizontal cylinder at the left. It pushes and pulls the connecting rod, which turns the flywheel. The heavy flywheel smooths out the motion of the piston to produce a steady action. Large steam engines today are usually turbines, not piston engines. Diesel engines and electric motors have replaced steam for many uses.

▼How James Watt's steam engine worked. The slide valve allowed steam into the cylinder first above, then below the piston. So that the piston was pushed first down, then up. In the condenser used steam from the cylinder was cooled and turned into water. A pump, driven by the engine, returned the water to the boiler. If the engine ran too fast or too slow, the governor altered the amount of steam going to the cylinder. The piston was connected to a rocking beam, which was connected to a flywheel. The continuously turning flywheel gave the rocking beam a smooth, regular action. The up and down motion of the beam could be used for pumping water, or the rotary motion of the flywheel could be used for driving machinery.

An *engine* is a device that releases *energy* from fuel. Energy is simply the ability to do work. For example, coal contains stored energy. Burning coal generates heat, which can be used to heat water and turn it into steam. The steam tries to expand, and can be made to turn wheels. So the steam engine releases the stored energy of the coal and uses it to do work that is useful to human beings.

It is, however, only during the last 300 years or so that human beings have learned how to build engines to help them in their work. The first engines were simple steam engines used for pumping water out of coal mines. Now mining and other industries are assisted by many kinds of engine. And most modern transport uses engines in place of muscle power.

Steam engines

The steam engine described above was invented by the Scottish engineer James Watt. He built it in 1783. It was not the first steam engine but it was an enormous improvement over earlier types. The piston in Watt's engine was a flat metal disc that could slide up and down in a metal cylinder (left). Steam under pressure from a boiler was led into a cylinder on one side of the piston. The steam expanded and pushed the piston to

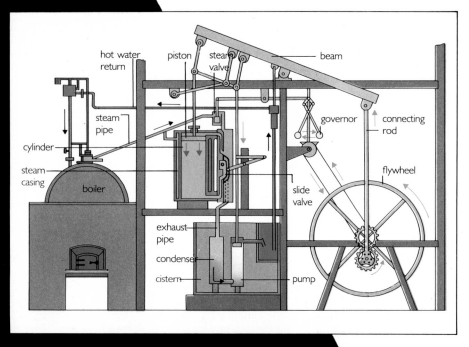

hot water return — piston — steam valve — beam
steam pipe
cylinder —
steam casing — boiler — governor — connecting rod
flywheel
slide valve
exhaust pipe
condenser
cistern — pump

one end of the cylinder. As it did so, a sliding valve automatically cut off the supply of steam to that side of the piston and instead led it in on the far side. The result was that the steam now started to push the piston back. At the end of each stroke the 'dead' steam was led away so that it would not resist the return movement of the piston. It passed to a chamber that was surrounded by cold water. Here the steam cooled down and condensed – turned back into water. This water was returned to the boiler to be used again.

The piston was connected to a rod that in turn was connected to a heavy flywheel. As the rod went back and forth, the flywheel turned. The flywheel's weight helped to give the piston a smooth action.

The steam engine transformed the lives of people in England, where it was first used, and then throughout the world. It improved the pumping of water, so that coal mines could go deeper than ever before. It replaced horses, which until then had been the most important source of power apart from human muscles. (The power of all types of engine is still measured in 'horse-power' – the number of horses that would have the same power.) Steam was used to drive looms, so that textiles could be woven faster and more cheaply than ever before. It was used to drive all sorts of other machinery too. More and more people worked in factories, where there was steam-driven machinery, and more and more of them began to live in towns where they could be close to the factories. Fewer workers were needed on the land, as steam-driven machinery took over from horses and human beings there. And, of course, the steam engine was put on wheels to make the first locomotives. At first these were used only in coal mines, to haul coal trucks. But soon the first passenger trains were in operation.

Steam engines were used in some of the earliest motor vehicles, too. Steam carriages were in regular use in Britain by the mid-nineteenth century. But efficient steam cars were not developed until later in the century – and by then they were in competition with the internal combustion engine.

▲Travel and transport were revolutionized when the steam engine was put on wheels to make the first railway locomotive. This is George Stephenson's *Rocket*. The first really practical locomotive, it was built in 1829. Its success was due to important details such as improvements in the firebox and the way steam was removed.

▲A steam-driven carriage of 1829, which travelled from London to Bath in 9 hours 20 minutes. There was great opposition to steam vehicles at first. A law was passed making it compulsory for a man carrying a red flag to walk in front of a mechanical vehicle. Steam-powered cars began to become efficient at the end of the 19th century – just as the petrol engine came into use.

Internal combustion engines

In a steam engine the fuel is burned outside the cylinder in which the piston moves. In a car engine, fuel is burned *inside* the cylinder, and the hot gases formed expand and move the piston. So the 'combustion' – burning – is 'internal' – inside.

Many different types of internal combustion engine were invented in the nineteenth century. Some burned coal gas, the same type of gas that was used for lighting and heating homes. But petrol (or gasoline) proved to be the best kind of fuel. It is obtained from oil that occurs naturally underground. The oil is a mixture of liquids, ranging from a heavy dark sludge to a light clear liquid that burns easily and makes a good fuel. The engines used in modern cars usually have four, six or eight cylinders. The cylinders may be vertical and in a straight line. Or they may be in pairs, tilted to form a series of Vs. These engines are of the 'four-stroke' type. This means that each piston makes four strokes – two upward and two downward movements – while burning one small quantity of fuel.

To understand how this type of engine works, we will follow the movements of one piston. Suppose that the engine is already running, and that the piston is just starting a downward movement. (The

▲An engine built by Gottlieb Daimler in 1885 in Germany. He used it to power a motorcycle built of wood. It was a four-stroke engine and was one of the forerunners of the modern car engine.

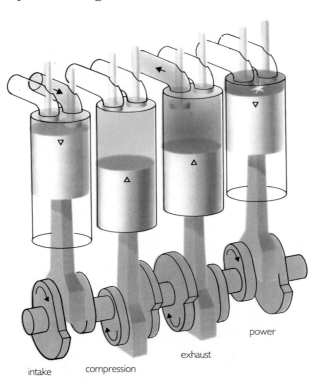

◀How a four-stroke engine works. A fuel inlet and an exhaust pipe go to the top of each cylinder, and are opened and closed by valves controlled by the motion of the pistons. The fuel-air mixture is drawn in during one of the piston's downward movements (the 'intake' stroke). The mixture is squeezed into a small space as the piston rises during the compression stroke. An electric spark ignites the mixture, and the hot gases produced push the piston down in the power stroke. Finally the piston rises again, pushing out the burnt gases in the exhaust stroke.

intake compression exhaust power

piston is joined to a shaft connected, through other shafts, to the wheels, so the movement of the car keeps the piston moving even at times when no petrol (gasoline) is being burned in that cylinder.)

As the piston moves down, it leaves behind it a vacuum – a space containing no air or other gas. But a mixture of air and petrol (gasoline) vapour rushes in to fill the gap above the piston. The mixture comes from a device called the carburetor, which mixes fuel and air in the right amounts.

The piston reaches the bottom of the cylinder and is then forced back up again by the continuing movement of the car. As it does so, it compresses (squeezes) the fuel-air mixture into a small space at the top of the cylinder. Compressing the mixture makes it burn better.

When the piston is at the top of its stroke, the fuel-air mixture is ignited (set alight) by an electric spark. There is an explosion that pushes the piston down. This small push is passed to the wheels, keeping the car moving.

In the last stage of the four-stroke action, the piston moves upwards again, this time pushing the burnt gases out of the cylinder. They are passed out through the exhaust pipe.

Each of the engine's cylinders fires in turn. The shaft they are connected to is called the crankshaft. It drives the wheels through a series of gears (page 33).

The first practical motor car using a petrol (gasoline) engine was built by the German engineer Karl Benz in 1885. In the same year his fellow countryman Gottlieb Daimler built a motorcycle powered by petrol (gasoline). Later he went on to build cars that used this fuel, too. These vehicles used four-stroke engines based on the design of Nikolaus August Otto.

The two-stroke engine was invented earlier than the four-stroke engine. It produces less power for a given amount of fuel than the four-stroke engine, but is useful for lighter vehicles such as motorcycles, and devices like lawnmowers.

In the two-stroke engine, fresh mixture is drawn into the lower part of the cylinder while the piston is in the upper part. When the piston moves down, it sweeps the new mixture round through a side channel to fill the space above the piston. As the piston rises, the mixture is compressed. A spark ignites the mixture when the piston is at the top of its movement. As the piston moves down again, the burnt gases are forced out by the entry of fresh mixture.

The diesel engine

Yet another kind of engine invented in the late nineteenth century was the diesel

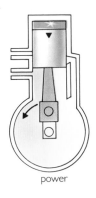  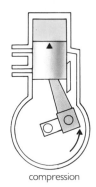

power exhaust intake compression

▲In two-stroke engines the space beneath the cylinder is called the crankcase, since it contains the crankshaft, which the piston turns. Fuel-air mixture is drawn into the crankcase while the piston is at the top of the cylinder. The mixture is ignited by a spark, and the explosion pushes the piston down. As it descends, it uncovers the exhaust outlet. As the piston nears the bottom of its stroke, fresh mixture is swept out of the crankcase into the cylinder, pushing out the last of the burnt gases. As the piston rises, it compresses the fresh mixture, ready for the electric spark.

▶A two-stroke engine for a powerboat. It is mounted at the stern, with its propeller just below the water, and is detachable. It has three horizontal cylinders. The pistons drive a shaft that is visible running down the middle of the engine. Water is pumped around the engine to cool it, and exhaust gases escape underwater.

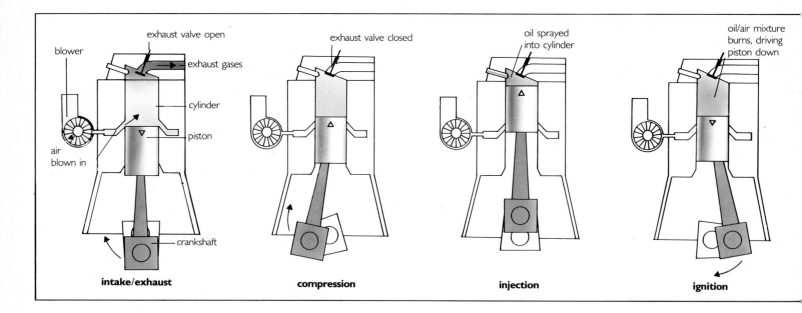

| blower | exhaust valve open | exhaust valve closed | oil sprayed into cylinder | oil/air mixture burns, driving piston down |

exhaust gases
cylinder
piston
air blown in
crankshaft

intake/exhaust **compression** **injection** **ignition**

▲The diesel engine's operating cycle. Air is blown into the cylinder under high pressure while the piston is near the bottom of its downward stroke. The incoming air pushes out the burnt gases from the previous ignition. As the piston rises, the air inlet and the exhaust are closed. The air is compressed so strongly that it becomes intensely hot. Fuel oil is sprayed in and instantly ignites. The piston is driven down, and the cycle is repeated.

▲A transcontinental diesel-powered train crosses a road in the Rocky Mountains of Canada. Diesel engines run on cheaper grades of oil than other kinds of engine. But they are heavier and more expensive to make. In locomotives, the diesel engine is normally used to make electricity, which drives a motor that turns the wheels.

engine. It is named after a German, Rudolf Diesel, who improved the design of the engine's British inventor, Herbert Akroyd Stuart. In a diesel engine, air above the piston is compressed very strongly and becomes very hot. (Gases always get hotter when compressed. A bicycle pump gets hot while it is being used because at each stroke some air is compressed.) Fuel is injected into this hot air and the mixture immediately ignites. The fuel used is obtained from oil, but is a denser part of it than petrol (gasoline). (This means that a given volume of it weighs more than the same volume of petrol or gasoline.) Diesel fuel is cheaper than petrol (gasoline). Railway locomotives, heavy lorries, trucks, ships and some cars have diesel engines.

Many other types of engine have been invented and are hard at work in the modern world. There are the jet engines that power aircraft (page 9). There are the rocket engines that drive spacecraft (page 18). And there are also electric motors. The word 'motor' is usually applied to a device that, though it produces movement of some kind, does not burn fuel to do so. An electric motor is powered by electricity. The electricity may come from a power station (where fuel was used in generating it). Or it may come from an engine. Railway locomotives are often 'diesel-electric'. A diesel engine is used to generate electricity, and this current drives an electric motor that turns the wheels (page 25).

Internal combustion engines are noisy and dirty. The exhaust gases they produce are poisonous. Cars driven by electric batteries would be quieter and cleaner. But they would also be slower and more expensive. Nevertheless, if oil were to become very expensive in the future, internal combustion engines might begin to give way to the electric motor.

MACHINES

Do you think you could lift your family car? perhaps you think that would be impossible – but you'd find it quite easy if you used the car's jack. A jack is a device that you place under the car. It has a platform or perhaps some kind of hook that you can raise by turning a handle or by moving a lever backwards and forwards repeatedly. As the jack rises, it lifts the car. You could even lift the largest truck with the aid of a jack.

A jack turns the comparatively weak force of human muscles into a force big enough to lift something weighing tonnes. A device that can do this is called a *machine*. We use countless machines in everyday life. The gears on a bicycle or in a car alter the force that is applied to the wheels. To pedal a bike uphill, a large force is needed to turn the back wheel. On

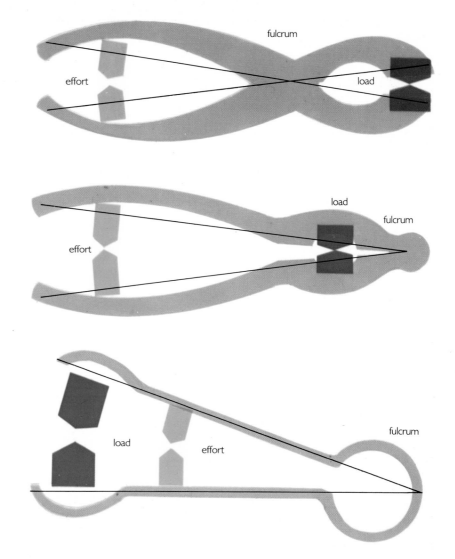

▲Three machines that you may have in your home. A pair of pliers (top) consists of two levers pivoted together. (The pivot is called the fulcrum.) A small effort applied to the handles results in a larger force (load) at the pincer end. A pair of nutcrackers (middle) also consists of two pivoted levers, but the load lies between the effort and the fulcrum. Again a small effort moving through a large distance results in a large force moving through a small distance. The sugar tongs (bottom) are an unusual type of machine – they reduce force instead of increasing it. This is because the effort is applied between the load and the levers' fulcrum, and so moves through a smaller distance than the load.

▲How gear wheels are used to change forces by changing turning speeds. (Top) The small gear wheel has 12 teeth, while the large one has 24. If a motor turns the small gear once, the large gear makes only half a turn – but it can exert a turning force twice as great as the smaller gear. In a bicycle (bottom) the rider's feet turn a large cogwheel. A chain runs over this and over the smaller hub of the rear wheel. Each turn of the rider's feet makes the rear wheel turn several times. This means the cyclist's feet can circle more slowly than the rear wheel, which is a more comfortable rate. When the cyclist changes gear, the chain is transferred to a rear wheel hub of different size. This changes the force with which the cyclist has to pedal.

◄Using a windlass, a worker can move a load that is too heavy to move unaided. The axle is turned by means of the spokes on top. In this case the length of a spoke is three times the radius of the axle. So when the effort moves through a certain distance, the load moves only one third as far. This means that the effort can move a load three times as great as itself.

▲This giant dragline excavator is a complex piece of equipment that contains many different kinds of machine – that is, devices for altering forces or sending them from one place to another. It is made up of a system of pulleys, levers and gears (all of which are types of machine), powered by a motor. This arrangement transfers the force supplied by the motor to the end of the cable attached to the load. It also increases the force and changes its direction.

a bike without gears, you would have to push the pedals harder. But on a bike with gears, you simply switch to 'low' gear, which increases the force applied to the rear wheel. You don't have to push the pedals any harder – though you *do* have to turn them faster.

A lever is a machine, since it can help us move things we couldn't otherwise move. You can use a stick to lever up a heavy paving stone, for example. You push one end of the lever down a long way in order to make the much heavier paving stone move upwards a small amount.

In factories, one man can easily lift heavy equipment with the aid of a pulley. This consists of a rope passing over an arrangement of wheels. As the worker pulls down on the rope, the load is raised. Although the worker has to pull down a great deal of rope to raise the load a little way and probably finds the task quite heavy, without the pulley he'd be unable

to shift the equipment.

Machines not only increase (or sometimes decrease) forces – they also 'transmit' them from one place to another and change their direction. The braking system in a car is an example of a machine. The driver presses the brake pedal with a comparatively weak force. The fluid in the brake pipes transmits the force to the brakes on the four wheels. The system is arranged so that the force is greatly increased and the brakes are applied hard.

The devices mentioned here all change forces in some way. Because, strictly speaking, only the kinds of devices that alter or transmit forces are machines. But we often use the word 'machine' for computers, clocks, television sets and so on. These do not change or transmit forces – they change or transmit information and so are not really machines.

Work, force and effort

You may have noticed that, in all the examples of machines that we have discussed so far, there is a price to pay for the increase in force. It is necessary to move the effort – the applied force – through a greater distance than the load moves. In raising a car with a jack you have to move your hand a long way – by turning a handle many times or pulling a lever backwards and forwards many times. When you use a pulley, you have to pull a long section of rope down with many hand-over-hand movements to raise the load a little way.

When you push or pull something and it moves, scientists say that you 'do work'. So in lifting a book from the table to a shelf, you do work. The heavier the book, and the farther you lift it, the more work you do. (If you push hard against a wall for five minutes, you'll get tired – but you won't have been doing any work in this special scientific sense!) When you use a machine to lift a heavy weight, you have to do just as much work as you would without the machine. You apply a smaller force but you move it through a larger distance – and with luck you get a better result!

All sorts of machines

You might be surprised at some of the everyday tools and other contrivances that scientists describe as machines. One of the simplest devices for raising heavy weights is the inclined plane. (A plane is a flat surface; 'inclined' means 'sloping'.) The massive stones used in building the Egyptian Pyramids or Stonehenge in Britain were probably dragged into position up long sloping ramps. The inclined plane is a machine in the scientific sense.

A screw is like an inclined plane that has been wound round and round a cylinder. The 'inclined plane' is called the screw's 'thread'. One type of car jack uses an upright screw. The user turns a handle, which rotates the screw and the car is forced upwards on the screw's thread.

An ordinary woodscrew is a machine, too. The effort you apply is the force with which you twist the screwdriver. The load

▲The spanner or wrench is a type of lever. The load is the resistance acting on the nut that is being turned. As the hand moves the lever, the load moves a much smaller distance, and so can be much greater than the effort applied by the hand.

is the resistance of the wood. Each time the screw turns, it moves forward just a little way into the wood. So the small turning force of your wrist can overcome the large resistance of the wood.

A pair of nutcrackers is a machine. They are designed so that, as you close them, your fingers move a greater distance than the pincers. The pincers exert a greater force than your fingers can.

But machines are not only used to boost human muscle power. Gears are used in cars and other motor vehicles. Pulley wheels are essential in cranes, which are used in factories, docks, mines and quarries. And *hydraulic* systems, which use oil or other fluids to transmit and alter force, are used in a huge variety of equipment, too. So machines help to multiply and control the force delivered by engines and other sources of energy.

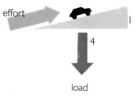

▲The effort that the car's engine must make to move the car up the slope of the hill is only a quarter of that needed to lift it to that height vertically. But the car must move four times as far. The work done – force times distance – is the same in both cases.

NUCLEAR ENERGY

Every year industry demands more and more energy – energy for manufacturing goods and materials. And every year ordinary people demand more energy – to heat and light their homes, run their cars and so on.

▲ The Atusha nuclear reactor in Argentina under construction. Notice the immensely thick walls which are typical of these reactors

A heavy spinning flywheel, a cylinder of high-pressure steam, and an electric battery are all said to contain energy. This means that they can all do useful work. The flywheel can be connected to machinery to drive it. At the same time the wheel slows down, so giving up its energy of movement. The steam can drive a piston, perhaps to pump water. As it does so, the steam cools down and its pressure falls – the steam loses energy. The battery can run an electric motor. Eventually the battery will 'go dead' and be unable to provide current – it will have lost its electrical energy.

The electricity used in homes and factories is generated in power stations by burning coal or oil. The heat is used to boil water, and the steam drives turbines that generate the electricity (page 25). Chemical energy in the coal or oil is turned into heat energy in the steam, and this is turned into electrical energy.

Part of the growing demand for energy is being met by nuclear energy. There is fierce argument about whether nuclear power stations are safe and necessary, but every industrialized country is building them. So what is nuclear energy?

When coal and oil burn, they combine with oxygen from the air. Their atoms – the tiny particles of which they are made – link up with atoms of oxygen. And in doing this they release energy that appears as heat.

Nuclear energy comes from atoms too. But it does not come from chemical reactions – from atoms joining up or separating from each other. It comes from the central part, the nucleus, of certain atoms.

At the heart of a nuclear power station is a reactor. It contains fuel in the form of rods, which can be lowered into the reactor and lifted out when the time comes to replace the fuel. The fuel is either uranium or plutonium. Uranium occurs naturally in rocks beneath the Earth's surface. Most uranium is of a type scientists call uranium 238, or U-238 for short. This means that the U-238 nucleus is made up of 238 smaller particles, called *protons* and *neutrons*. A small fraction of

◄Enriched uranium is not necessarily the most powerful source of nuclear energy. Research is already being carried out on accelerator neutron reactors. Some, using liquid sodium, are 87 times more powerful than enriched uranium ones.

all uranium atoms are of a different type. These are called U-235 because the nucleus in their atoms contains 235 particles. Only the U-235 atoms provide nuclear energy, so some of the U-238 is removed from natural uranium to make it suitable for fuel. This is called 'enriching' the uranium.

Uranium atoms are 'unstable' – they split up, or decay. And some neutrons from the original nucleus are lost and travel off at high speed. Some radiation is given off, too. This means that uranium in the rocks can be discovered by the radiation given out by decaying atoms. U-235 atoms are much more likely to split up than U-238 atoms are.

When a uranium atom has split, the neutrons given out travel on until they collide with the nuclei of other atoms and are absorbed. In natural uranium, a neutron is unlikely to strike a U-235 nucleus. But in the enriched uranium used in reactors, there is much more U-235 present, and a collision with a U-235 nucleus is therefore much more likely.

When it is struck by a neutron, a U-235 nucleus splits in two – scientists call this nuclear *fission*. And if one of the neutrons

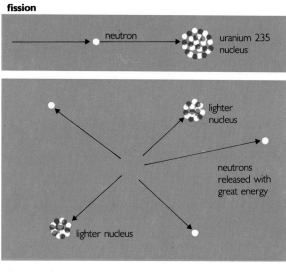

fission

neutron → uranium 235 nucleus

lighter nucleus

neutrons released with great energy

lighter nucleus

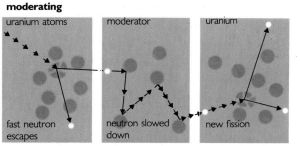

moderating

uranium atoms — moderator — uranium

fast neutron escapes — neutron slowed down — new fission

◄How nuclear fission works. A nucleus of uranium 235 – which is just one kind of uranium – is made up of 235 protons and neutrons. If a neutron strikes the nucleus, it splits into two lighter nuclei, and sends out neutrons and radiation. If the uranium is rich enough in U-235, the newly produced neutrons will strike other U-235 nuclei, causing them to split, and there will be a chain reaction.

▲Fission (the splitting of a nucleus into two parts) is inefficient if the neutrons move too fast. To slow them down, another material, called a moderator, is placed among the fuel rods. Neutrons escaping from fuel rods bounce off the atoms of the moderator, enter the fuel again, and have a good chance of causing fission. Coolant water acts as the moderator in one type of reactor.

it sends out strikes another U-235 nucleus, that one will split too. A chain reaction is set up, with each splitting triggering off the splitting of other nuclei. If the chain reaction runs out of control, millions upon millions of nuclei will split in a fraction of a second, pouring out heat and radiation. This is what happens in a nuclear explosion. But in a reactor, there are ways of controlling the chain reaction. Among the fuel rods there are 'control' rods made of a material that absorbs neutrons. When the control rods are fully lowered into the reactor, they absorb so many neutrons that a chain reaction cannot be set up. As they are gradually raised out of the reactor, neutrons escaping from a fuel rod are able to travel on and enter other fuel rods, where they may cause splitting. So the chain reaction runs at a controlled rate.

The uranium becomes extremely hot. This heat is removed and put to work. This is done with a 'coolant', which may be water kept at high pressure to prevent it from boiling, or it may be a gas. The coolant is passed through pipes immersed in water. This water boils and the steam is used to generate electricity.

The U-235 in the fuel rods is gradually used up, and 'fission products' accumulate.

These are the substances produced as the U-235 atoms split. They absorb neutrons and so tend to slow the reaction down. The fuel rods are removed after a period of use and sent for 'reprocessing'. The waste products are removed, and unused U-235 is recovered to be made into new fuel rods.

There is, however, another substance in the used fuel rods – plutonium. This is made when neutrons are absorbed by U-238. It is an artificial element, which did not exist on Earth until it was created in the first nuclear reactor. And it, too, can be used as fuel in reactors.

Plutonium is used, together with uranium, in a special kind of reactor called a 'breeder' reactor. Neutrons from the plutonium turn still more U-238 into plutonium. And this plutonium provides heat just as uranium does in an ordinary reactor.

The waste products from nuclear reactors pose a great problem. They are deadly because they are highly *radioactive* – that is, they send out intense radiations that can cause sickness and death. Because radioactivity will last for centuries, the wastes have to be sealed in some shielding material and buried, or

dumped on the ocean floor.

This is one aspect of nuclear energy that worries many people. Another is the possibility of an accident in which the reactor overheats, melts and releases radioactive substances into the atmosphere, with disastrous effects on people downwind.

But safety precautions are so stringent that such an accident is extremely unlikely. And in normal operation, a nuclear plant causes hardly any pollution – unlike coal and oil-fired power stations, which continually pour out smoke and dust that contribute to thousands of deaths every year.

So, though the debate about nuclear energy goes on, so does the building of new reactors.

▲Two engineers checking the control rods of a nuclear reactor. These contain a material that absorbs neutrons. When they are inserted into the reactor, they shut off the chain reaction.

39

TURBINE

Turbines are engines in which the moving parts rotate, and are driven by a gas or liquid that flows through the turbine. In a power station, steam is used to drive giant turbines. The rotating turbine drives electrical generators, producing electrical power.

A toy windmill gives a good idea of how a turbine works. The blades of the windmill are shaped so that, when the wind strikes them, they turn. In a turbine, there are often many sets of turbine blades. Each set is called a rotor. When a fluid – steam, hot gas or water – flows through the turbine, it has to pass through each rotor in turn. Between one rotor and the next there may be a stator – a set of fixed blades that guide the fluid to make sure it hits the next set of rotor blades at the best angle.

Powerful engines

A widely-known type of turbine is the turbojet that powers jet aircraft. The fuel burnt in a turbojet engine produces hot gases at high pressure, which escapes from the rear of the engine. As this jet of hot gas escapes, the engine receives a forward push (page 9). On its way out of the engine, the hot gases pass through several sets of turbine blades. These are mounted on a shaft that runs the length of the engine. As the rotors turn, the shaft turns. At the front end of the shaft there are sets of 'compressor' blades. As they turn they suck in air at the front of the engine and compress (squeeze) it. Then the air is mixed with fuel. Compressing the air makes the fuel burn better and release more of its energy.

Other types of turbine-powered aircraft are not jets. The hot gases from the burning fuel do not shoot out of the back of the engine in a stream, pushing the engine forward. Nearly all the energy of the gases is used up in turning the turbine. In turn, the turbine drives propellers that throw air backwards and so pull the aircraft forward through the air. This is a 'turboprop' engine – in other words an engine powered by turbine-driven propellers. (There are also turbofan engines, which power jumbo jets. They are a kind of combination of jet and turboprop engines.)

Gas turbines are used in some fast boats to drive the propellers. And gas turbines are used in some power stations to drive electrical generators for short times when there is a heavy demand for

▼The blades of a gas turbine that has had its outer casing removed. The sizes and angles of all the blades are carefully chosen to make sure that the maximum amount of energy is extracted from the hot gases that drive the turbine. Gas turbines are used to drive aircraft and ships, and to generate electricity.

◄An aircraft's jet engine under construction. The air intake is at the bottom of the picture. The air is sucked in and compressed by the first series of blades. Then fuel is mixed with the air and burned. The hot gases produced pass through the turbine blades (dark colour) and make them rotate. Then the gases escape at the rear of the engine, pushing it forward. The turbine blades and compressor blades are mounted on the same shaft, so as the turbine rotates, the compressor blades do too.

▼A water turbine in a hydro-electric power station. A jet of high-pressure water from a reservoir or a mountain river passes through the turbine, making it spin. The turbine is connected to an electricity generator.

electricity. Gas turbines have been used to power some experimental cars, but in the future they are likely to be used only in large vehicles, such as long-distance buses. Some cars have 'Turbo' in their names, meaning that their engines are 'turbocharged'. A small turbine compresses air and forces it into the engine to burn the fuel more efficiently than in an ordinary engine. The turbine is driven by the engine's exhaust gases.

EXPLOSIVE

An explosion occurs when gases expand violently, pushing against the surrounding matter. The gases are formed from a solid or liquid, or from other gases, by a rapid chemical reaction. For example, cars are driven by a series of explosions. A small amount of petrol vapour is burned in one of the engine cylinders. Hot gases are formed that expand and push down a piston. This happens repeatedly in all the engine's cylinders, and the movement of the pistons turns the car's wheels.

An explosive is a substance that is used to produce explosions. It can be of two kinds. It may produce a large volume of gas very quickly, causing a destructive, shattering explosion. Or it may create a slower, less violent explosion, which can be used for propulsion. Both types are found in a missile – there is propellant explosive to drive it, and a more violent, shattering explosive in the warhead.

Gunpowder was the first explosive to be made. We do not know exactly when and where it was invented, but the Chinese were using it in warfare by the tenth century AD. They used it in rockets like our modern firework rockets. By 1300 gunpowder was being used by Arab armies, in guns that fired arrows rather than bullets.

The secret of making gunpowder probably reached Europe about this time. It was a mixture of sulphur, charcoal and saltpetre. Firearms soon replaced the bow in European warfare.

The work of the Nobels

In the nineteenth century other forms of explosive were developed. An Italian chemist, Ascanio Sobrero, invented nitroglycerine in 1846. The slightest vibration would make it explode. In 1866 a Swedish father and son, Immanuel and Alfred Nobel, found a safe way of manufacturing nitroglycerine. Then Alfred Nobel combined it with other materials to make dynamite, which was safer to handle because it needed a detonator – a small explosive charge – to make it explode.

Another powerful explosive, TNT (trinitrotoluene) was invented in 1863. Like dynamite, it needed a detonator to make it explode.

Nobel made a fortune from his explosives. He used some of the money to set up his famous Nobel Prizes, still awarded every year for outstanding contributions to chemistry, physics, medicine, literature and peace. Nobel, a life-long opponent of war, believed that the new explosives were so destructive that they would make large-scale warfare impossible. He was tragically wrong: immense devastation was caused in the two World Wars by artillery barrages and bombing from the air, using yet more powerful explosives.

Nuclear explosives

Nuclear weapons – atomic bombs and hydrogen bombs – dwarf the explosive power of all previous explosives. The destructive power of an atomic bomb is measured in 'kilotonnes'; one kilotonne is the explosive power of 1,000 tonnes of TNT. And the power of the hydrogen bomb is measured in megatonnes – equivalent to *millions* of tonnes of TNT.

Useful explosions

Explosives have many peaceful uses. They are used to blast away rock in quarries and mines, so that valuable ores can be extracted. Small explosive charges separate the different stages of spacecraft. Even nuclear explosives may one day be used to dig holes for canals and ports. Explosives are used to demolish buildings that are no longer needed. And small explosive charges are set off by geologists (scientists who study the Earth) in order to send shock waves deep into the ground. By recording the vibrations of the ground produced by the explosions – miniature artificial earthquakes – the geologists learn about the different types of rock underground. Often, for example, they can discover oil in this way.

▶An idea for a perpetual motion machine, from a 17th-century book. Falling water drives a water wheel, which turns a grindstone. It also turns a spiral screw that lifts water to the upper reservoir. The machine could not run for ever because it would lose energy, which is not replaced.

Imagine a water mill beside a lake at the foot of a mountain. The mill grinds wheat to make flour and also pumps water up the mountainside to a reservoir. Water flows down a channel from the reservoir to the lake. As it does so, it turns the water mill, which grinds wheat – and pumps water up the mountainside. . . .

machine – a machine that could run for an unlimited time, doing useful work, without any interference from outside. But perpetual motion machines are impossible.

Inventors have been designing ingenious perpetual motion machines for hundreds of years, and every year new simply its ability to do work of some kind. The water in the reservoir has 'potential' energy – because it is high up the mountainside it has the ability to do work, such as turning the mill, simply by being allowed to flow downhill to a lower place.

When the water flows downhill, it loses its potential energy, but this is turned into 'kinetic' energy – energy of movement – for the moving water can do work in turning the mill. Different forms of energy can appear and disappear, but the total amount of all kinds of energy is conserved – that is, stays the same.

When, say, one tonne of water has flowed downhill, turning the mill, another tonne of water has to be pumped up to the reservoir to replace it. And it has to be given exactly the same amount of potential energy that the first tonne of water has lost in flowing down. There is no energy left over to grind the wheat or do anything else. Only if energy is provided from outside can the mill both pump the water back up the mountainside *and* grind the wheat.

Overbalancing wheels

Many suggested perpetual motion machines have used the principle of the 'overbalancing wheel'. Weights were to be attached to a wheel in such a way that it was unbalanced and would start to turn. The weights would shift as the wheel turned, keeping it constantly unbalanced. The wheel could be connected to machinery, which could run for ever – or at least until it wore out.

But this too breaks the law of conservation of energy. As the weights move down on one side of the wheel, they lose potential energy. As they rise on the other side, they must be given back exactly the same amount of potential energy. This cannot happen if the wheel is doing work, and so the wheel will come to a stop.

A patent impossibility!

When someone invents a new device or process, he or she can apply for a 'patent'. This prevents anyone else using the new invention unless they have the inventor's permission – for which they must usually pay a fee. Every year people try to get patents on their ideas for perpetual motion machines. The British Patent Office refuses such applications automatically. The United States Patent Office will grant a patent – provided it is shown a working model of the machine. But no one ever produces one!

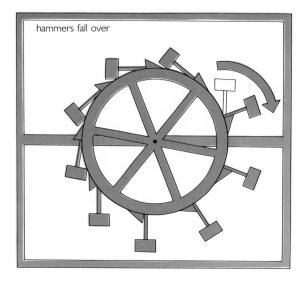

hammers fall over

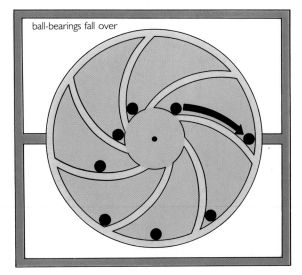

ball-bearings fall over

◄An 'overbalancing wheel' of the 13th century. The weights are at the ends of hinged arms. On one side of the wheel the arms lie flat against the rim. On the other, they project. The idea was that the projecting weights would drag the wheel round. As the wheel turned, further weights would swing out, keeping it turning. But in fact the downward forces on the two sides would just balance.

◄In this variant of the overbalancing wheel, the balls at the right are farther from the middle than those on the left. The inventor thought the wheel would overbalance to the right. But though the balls on the left are closer to the middle, there are more of them, and the wheel is balanced.

◄In this device water is supposed to be raised by the screw at the left. The screw consists of a spiral tube wound around a shaft, which is turned by gear wheels driven by the water wheel. The wheel is turned by the water falling onto it from the top of the screw. This machine, too, would rapidly come to a stop.

EXTENDING OUR SENSES

GEIGER COUNTER

Radioactivity cannot be seen, heard or felt – but it can do deadly harm to living things. Therefore it is very important to be able to tell when there is radioactivity around. The Geiger counter is a widely used radioactivity detector. It was developed from devices invented in the

▼Using a Geiger counter to detect radioactive materials.

early twentieth century by Johannes Geiger and Ernest Rutherford.

There are three kinds of radioactivity. Alpha rays consist of helium nuclei – the central parts of helium atoms. They carry positive electric charges. Beta rays consist of fast-moving electrons – tiny particles carrying negative electric charges. Gamma rays are similar to the X-rays used by doctors. The Geiger counter is best at detecting alpha rays. It consists of a glass tube containing the gas argon at low pressure. There is a metal cylinder along the length of the tube, and a metal wire running along the centre of the cylinder.

The wire and the cylinder are connected

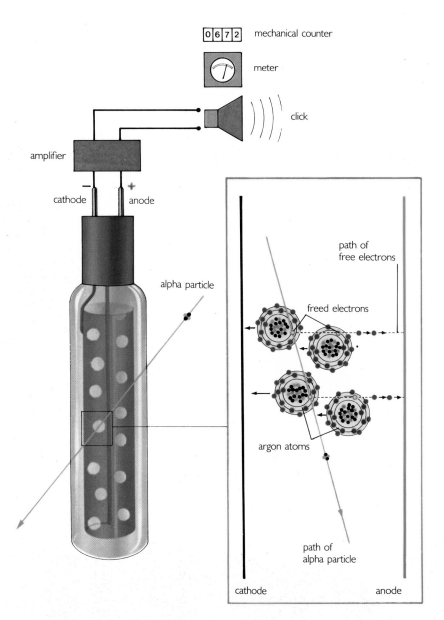

mechanical counter

meter

click

amplifier

cathode anode

alpha particle

path of free electrons

freed electrons

argon atoms

path of alpha particle

cathode anode

◄A Geiger counter can react to a single alpha particle (which makes up one kind of radioactivity). The atoms of argon gas in the counter (see inset) contain electrons (grey dots) in their outer layers. Some of these electrons are knocked out of their atoms when an alpha particle speeds through. The electrons are negatively charged, and are drawn to the positively charged wire

(anode) in the middle of the counter. The incomplete argon atoms have a positive electric charge, which is no longer cancelled out by the electrons they have lost. These atoms drift towards the negatively charged cylinder (cathode). The tiny momentary current is amplified to register on a counter or a meter, or to be heard as a click from a loudspeaker.

to opposite terminals of a battery. The battery tries to drive an electric current between the wire and the cylinder, but it cannot pass through the argon gas.

Alpha particles however can pass through glass. If one enters the Geiger counter, it knocks fragments off the argon atoms it collides with. These fragments are electrons and electric currents consist of streams of electrons.

The central wire is connected to the battery's positive terminal. Positive voltages attract negative electric charges, so the electrons are drawn to the wire and flow along it to the battery. This is a short burst of electric current, which is heard as a click from a loudspeaker, or shown as a movement of a needle, or recorded by a counting device.

Another type of detector

The Geiger counter is not always the best instrument for measuring radioactivity. For example, the workers in a nuclear power plant may be at danger if they are exposed to weak radioactivity over a long period. It is the total amount of radioactivity that they are exposed to that is important, and a Geiger counter does not measure this. Each worker wears a badge containing photographic film, protected from the light. Radioactivity affects the film just as light would. When the film is developed, the degree of 'fogging' or fuzziness on it shows how much radioactivity the wearer has been exposed to.

Whenever a sound recording is made, or a TV or radio programme is broadcast, or someone makes a telephone call, a microphone is being used. A microphone turns sound waves, which are vibrations of the air, into electrical signals, which are variations in the strength of an electric current. The electrical signal can be sent long distances along a cable or as radio or television waves, and can then be turned back into sound waves that are a copy of the original sound.

Telephones

A telephone handset has a microphone in the mouthpiece. There is a metal membrane (plate), which works rather like your eardrums. When sound waves strike the membrane, they make it vibrate. The membrane is mounted on a cone-shaped 'diaphragm'. Grains of carbon are packed behind the diaphragm. The vibrations of the membrane cause changes in the pressure on the carbon grains. These pressure changes cause the grains to be more tightly or more loosely packed together. An electric current constantly passes through the grains. When they are tightly packed, the current can pass easily. When they are less tightly packed, the current is reduced in strength. Its strength constantly changes, in just the same way as the strength of the sound waves made by the person speaking.

◄A ribbon microphone, used for high-quality recording. Inside it there is a metal ribbon in a magnetic field. Sound waves make the ribbon vibrate, creating an electric current that constantly changes in strength. The current is a 'copy' of the sound waves.

►This photograph shows the insides of an electrostatic microphone. At the top are two circular 'plates'. Sound waves make the distance between the plates change constantly. This sets up a varying electric current that is used for broadcasting or recording.

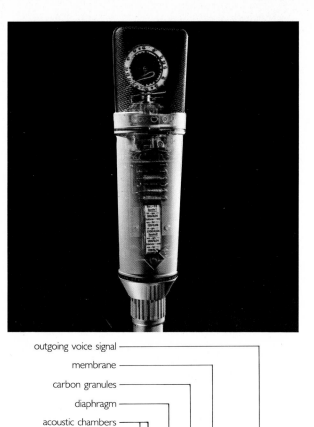

outgoing voice signal
membrane
carbon granules
diaphragm
acoustic chambers

▼These two photographs show just how far sound recording and reproduction have come in the years between the making of the Edison phonograph (**inset bottom**) and the Japanese sound system (**below**).

▲The microphone in a telephone mouthpiece. Sound waves make the metal membrane vibrate, and this makes the pressure on the carbon grains vary. And this in turn changes the strength of an electric current passing through the carbon. The current flows along the telephone wires to the earpiece of another telephone, where it makes another metal membrane vibrate and reproduce the original sounds.

The electric current passes along the telephone wires to the earpiece of the telephone at the other end of the line. There it makes another metal membrane vibrate. And these vibrations make sound waves that are a copy of the person's words, however great a distance the electric current has to travel.

Different types of microphone

There are many different types of microphone. In one type, sound waves make a metal ribbon vibrate in a magnetic field. The vibrations create the varying electric current. In other types, the sound waves strike a special crystal – possibly quartz. The changes in pressure produce the varying electric current.

The work of amplifiers

The current from a microphone is quite a weak one. It usually has to be passed to an amplifier – a device that makes it stronger – before it can be broadcast or recorded or used to drive a loudspeaker.

◄Without modern microphones, today's huge pop concerts would be impossible – no one near the back of an audience of thousands of people would be able to hear anything.

SUBMARINE

▲A nuclear submarine on the surface as it comes into harbour. It is carrying long-range missiles, which can be fired almost instantly in the event of war. Craft like this can stay on patrol for weeks or months without surfacing.

The submarine took its modern form in the last quarter of the nineteenth century. Before then, although there had been many attempts to make underwater boats, there had been no suitable engines. Some had used electric motors powered by batteries, because they did not need air, and so could operate underwater. But electric motors were not very powerful and the submarine could not travel far before it had to return to its base to recharge the batteries. An American inventor, John Holland, built several submarines and finally hit on the answer. He put a petrol (gasoline) engine and an electric motor together in one craft. The

engine, which needed air, could be used on the surface and could propel the vessel relatively fast. It could also charge up the electric motor, which could be used for the short periods in which the submarine was below the surface.

John Holland demonstrated this submarine in 1900. The world's navies immediately began building similar submarines, and they proved deadly in both world wars. These later submarines used diesel engines because diesel oil is very much easier to store safely in the confined space of a submarine. Most modern submarines use diesel-electric propulsion.

But in 1955 a new type of propulsion for submarines was introduced. This was nuclear ('atomic') power. A nuclear reactor containing uranium fuel generates heat that turns water into steam. The steam turns turbines connected to the submarine's propellers. The reactor needs no air and can run for years without being refuelled. So the submarine can stay submerged all this time, and is very difficult for an enemy to detect. One of the earliest nuclear submarines, the *Triton*, travelled round the world underwater in 1960.

How submarines work
A submarine consists of a very tough central section in which the crew live. This part has to be strong enough to resist the high pressure of the ocean depths. It is constructed from welded steel, with compartments separated by strong bulkheads (partitions). Surrounding this part are the ballast, or buoyancy, tanks. These tanks are filled with air while the submarine is on the surface. Sea water can be let into them, driving the air out and making the submarine heavier, so that it sinks. When the captain wishes to take the submarine to the surface again, compressed air from storage tanks is blown into the ballast tanks, driving out the water and making the craft lighter.

When the submarine is floating on the surface, it is said to have 'positive buoyancy'. When it is diving, it has

◄Modern submarines may not travel as fast as *Concorde*, but controlling them still requires highly complex technical equipment. Compare the control room of this submarine with the flight deck of *Concorde* on page 11.

'negative buoyancy'. And when it is travelling on a level course underwater, the amount of water in the flotation tanks is adjusted to give it 'neutral buoyancy' – it neither sinks nor rises. As it uses fuel, the submarine grows lighter and small 'trim tanks' are filled with water to adjust the buoyancy. The submarine's movements are controlled by small 'wings', called hydroplanes, at the front and rear, and by a rudder.

A submarine can travel just below the surface, hiding from enemies, while the captain scans the surface through his periscope. This is a tall tube mounted in the top of the submarine, containing a complex system of lenses and mirrors. It reflects a view of the scene above the surface down to the eyepiece in the submarine's control room. Diesel-electric craft are also fitted with a snorkel tube, which permits the diesel engines to run while the submarine is just below the surface. The snorkel contains an air intake and an exhaust.

Submersibles

Non-military submarines are usually small and are called 'submersibles'. They are used for underwater exploration by archeologists looking for ships that sank hundreds of years ago, or by scientists studying sea creatures. Repair work on sunken oil pipelines and telephone cables is often done with submersibles. The

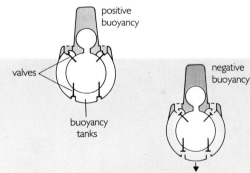

positive buoyancy

valves

buoyancy tanks

negative buoyancy

neutral buoyance

vessel may have robot arms on the front that can be operated by the crew. Some one-man submersibles are really bulky diving suits with mechanical limbs and built-in motors.

▲How a submarine is controlled. When its buoyancy tanks are filled with air, the submarine floats. It has 'positive buoyancy'. When the tanks are completely flooded with water, the submarine has 'negative buoyancy', and it dives. For underwater cruising a little of the water is forced out to give 'neutral buoyancy', which means that the submarine does not rise or sink.

◄Engineers give a Remote Maintenance Vehicle (RMV) a last test before it is lowered into the North Sea for routine maintenance and inspection of oil pipelines and other installations.

SPACE FLIGHT

The space age began when the first artificial *satellite*, or 'moon', was launched by the Soviet Union in 1957. It was an aluminium sphere less than 1 m (3 ft) across. It contained some scientific instruments and sent the results of their measurements back to Earth by radio, as a 'bleeping' sound. It was called *Sputnik*, from a Russian word meaning 'travelling companion'.

Previously, rockets had reached the fringes of space, over 150 km (93 miles) high, where the Earth's atmosphere is thinner than the best vacuum we can make in the laboratory. But when their engines stopped firing, the rockets fell back to Earth. *Sputnik* travelled so fast that it did not do this. Its powerful launch rocket boosted the satellite to a speed of just under 29,000 kph (18,000 mph). Then *Sputnik* separated from the launch rocket and coasted on. It did not need rocket

▼In pictures such as this Skylab looks very small. In fact it is as long as a 12-storey building is high. A second electricity-generating solar panel was ripped off during Skylab's launch.

engines of its own to keep it going. In the airlessness of space, there is no *friction* to bring a spacecraft to a stop.

But the Earth's gravitational pull prevented *Sputnik* from escaping, just as it prevents objects on the ground from flying off into space. It pulled the satellite's path into a closed orbit. ('Orbit' is the name for the path followed by a freely moving body in space, such as a planet or a spaceship with its engines turned off.) In just the same way, the Moon, Earth's natural satellite, is held in its orbit by the Earth's *gravitation*.

Sputnik's orbit was elliptical – that is, like a flattened circle. At its highest, the satellite was 934 km (580 miles) high. At its lowest it was only 224 km (139 miles) high. It took 1½ hours for the satellite to travel on its orbit around the Earth. At the lowest point it was slightly slowed by the drag of the thin traces of the Earth's atmosphere. After several months the satellite had been slowed down so much that it fell back into the atmosphere. The heat generated by friction as it fell through the air burned it up.

The first astronauts

An American satellite, Explorer 1, soon followed. At the same time both the Soviet Union and the United States were working on sending men into space. In April 1961 the Russian astronaut, Yuri Gagarin, made one complete orbit of the Earth. To return to Earth, he fired 'retro-rockets' – rockets that gave his space capsule a push in the opposite direction to the one he was travelling in. This reduced the capsule's speed so that it started to spiral towards the Earth. Once back in the atmosphere, friction slowed it even more. The capsule had a special heat-proof covering to prevent it burning up as Sputnik had done. Before the capsule hit the ground, Gagarin bailed out and came down by parachute. The following year the American astronaut, John Glenn, made three orbits of the Earth in a space capsule.

Unmanned satellites

Many more unmanned satellites were launched. Some were designed to study the Earth from space. They took

photographs of the Earth and then
returned the film to the ground by
parachute, or they carried TV cameras.
They observed weather patterns to
improve weather forecasting. Or they
studied the vegetation and rock
formations of remote areas to learn what
natural resources were present. Many
satellites were 'spies in the sky', studying
the military bases of the countries they
flew over. Some of the cameras on
satellites are so powerful that they can
show individual people on the ground.

Other satellites were intended for
peaceful scientific purposes. They studied
the radiations in space, or the tiny
particles of space dust, called micro-
meteoroids. Or they studied the infra-red
(heat) waves or X-rays from the Sun,
stars and planets – radiations that never
reach astronomers on Earth because our
atmosphere blocks them out.

Communications satellites
One of the most important uses of
satellites was for communications. Echo 1,
launched in 1960, was a giant plastic

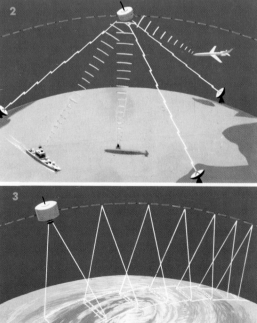

▲The Apollo 9 mission
in March 1969 was
mainly to test the
equipment that would
be used in the moon
landing. This
photograph of the
command module,
Gumdrop, was taken
from the lunar landing
vehicle.

◀Three of the many
uses of satellites. 1) 24-
hour satellites can
provide a radio and TV
link between
continents. 2) They can
help ships and planes
find their positions.
3) And they can
observe weather over
vast areas.

53

balloon coated with aluminium. It was inflated after it had been launched into orbit. Radio waves from the ground would be reflected from the balloon and could be received over a wide area. But the reflected signals were weak because they were scattered widely. Later comsats – communications satellites – had receivers and amplifying equipment on board. They would receive the radio or TV waves from the ground, amplify them – that is, make them stronger – and send them back in a beam that covered a definite area on the ground.

There was another important improvement in communications satellites. Nearly all of them are now sent into orbit exactly 35,880 km (22,300 miles) high. At this distance from the Earth, each satellite takes exactly 24 hours to make one orbit, moving from west to east. And this is exactly the

length of the day – the time it takes the Earth to rotate once from west to east. The result is that the satellite seems to stay fixed above one point on the Earth's equator. Earlier satellites in lower orbits sped across the sky, so the aerials on the ground had to be able to swing round to keep track of them. And the radio signal would be cut off when the satellite went below the horizon.

Now there are dozens of satellites in the 24-hour 'geostationary' orbit, relaying radio and TV broadcasts and telephone messages. Some satellites can relay 20,000 telephone conversations simultaneously. Most intercontinental telephone calls are made via satellite.

Exploring space
In the 1960s, while more and more satellites were put into orbit, some spacecraft were launched beyond Earth's

▼ A hurricane as seen from a satellite and monitored by the National Oceanic and Atmospheric Administration in Miami. The red area in the picture shows the area of densest cloud.

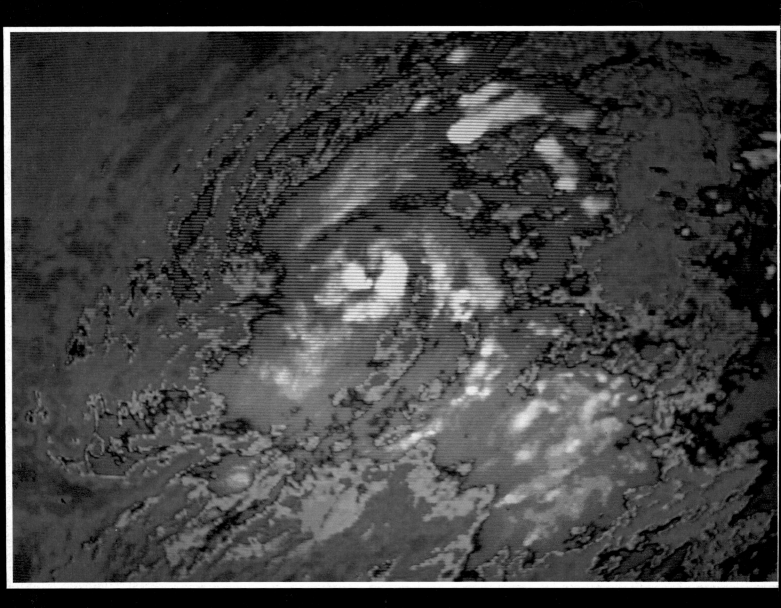

gravity, to the Moon, planets – and even out of the *solar system* completely. If a spacecraft is boosted to a speed of 40,000 kph (25,000 mph) and its engines are shut off, it will coast on for ever. It will gradually slow down as the Earth tries to pull it back, but it will never quite stop, for the Earth's gravity becomes so weak at great distances that it is almost non-existent. This speed is called 'escape velocity'.

▶'Earthrise', seen from an Apollo spacecraft in orbit around the Moon. The rocky, cratered surface of the Moon is clearly visible. The Moon has no atmosphere to protect its surface from meteors, cosmic rays and extremes of heat and cold.

▲Edwin (Buzz) Aldrin, the second man on the Moon, descends from the lunar landing craft Eagle. The photograph was taken by Neil Armstrong, the first man to set foot on the Moon.

◀Jim Irwin stands beside the lunar rover used on the Apollo 15 moon landing. The thing that looks like an upside-down umbrella is an antenna for beaming television and voice communications back to Earth.

The Russian spacecraft, Luna 2, was the first spacecraft to break free of Earth's gravity. It landed on the Moon in 1959. Then, in 1966, two unmanned craft made the first controlled landings on the Moon. These were the Russian Luna 9 and the American Surveyor 1.

Space 'probes' have also gone to the nearest planets. To travel to Venus, which is nearer to the Sun than the Earth is, a probe first goes into a 'parking' orbit around the Earth, sharing the Earth's motion around the Sun of 28 km (17 miles) per second. The probe, under radio control from the ground, then fires its rocket engines against the direction of the Earth's motion. As a result the probe travels around the Sun too slowly to stay in the same orbit and it falls inwards, towards the Sun and Venus. The orbit is very precisely calculated, so, after some weeks of travel, it is close to Venus. It may then go into orbit around Venus, and send information about the planet back to Earth by radio. Another type of probe may enter the planet's thick atmosphere, or else send out smaller probes to do this. Venus probes have discovered that the surface of Venus is hotter than boiling water and that the atmospheric pressure is crushing – a hundred times greater than the atmospheric pressure on Earth.

Space probes have also travelled outward from the Sun, to the outer planets. Mariner 4 travelled to Mars in 1964. First it went into a parking orbit around the Earth, sharing its motion around the Sun. Then it fired its engines to gain additional speed compared with the Earth. This caused it to move outwards, in a larger orbit than the Earth's. After eight months of travel, it reached Mars. It did not land, but took photographs and radioed them to Earth. Scientists were surprised to discover that Mars had a heavily *cratered* surface, similar to the Moon's, and that there were no signs of any flowing water.

The later Viking mission landed a completely automatic laboratory on Mars. The robot lab scraped up samples of the soil and carried out chemical tests in a search for simple life forms, such as bacteria. Its results were puzzling, but they did not seem to show any Martian life.

Other probes have flown past the huge planets Jupiter and Saturn, sending back spectacular pictures. Jupiter is a globe of gas that could swallow up a million Earths. The Voyager probes have sent back TV pictures of storms in its atmosphere that are larger than our planet and have lasted for centuries. The same probes have shown the complicated structure of the rings of Saturn, and are now continuing their journeys out of the solar system altogether.

Some scientists think that robot space probes are the best way of exploring space, because it is enormously expensive to keep human beings alive in space. There are no plans to repeat the half-dozen manned trips to the Moon, made between 1969 and 1972. But there *are* plans to set up permanent space stations in orbit around the Earth. There have already been experimental space stations – the huge American Skylab, which was manned for nearly six months, and the Soviet series of *Salyut* stations, which have been manned by different crews over periods of years.

Weightlessness

The crew members on space stations live in conditions of weightlessness. You have probably seen TV pictures of them, 'swimming' through the air, surrounded by floating items of equipment. On Earth we have a sensation of weight because the downward pull of gravity is resisted by the things that hold us up – the ground,

▼The surface of Mars was seen in detail for the first time by the Viking missions in July 1976. In the foreground of the picture part of Viking 2's soil sampler is just visible.

◀The surface of Jupiter, showing two of its moons: Europa on the right and Io above the planet's famous Red Spot.

▼In November 1980 Voyager 1 photographed Saturn's rings. This picture also shows the shadows the rings make on the surface of the planet and one of its moons.

▼A member of Skylab's crew inspects a space suit. Notice how the suit is kept in place with toe loops.

▲This shower used by the astronauts in Skylab was not a great success – a spray of water is apt to remain floating because there is no gravity – and it took up a lot of precious space.

▼No need for a dentist's chair – in space the patient just floats while his teeth are examined. Checks like this are important to see if life in space affects the human body.

▼One way of eating scrambled egg! One of the crew on the second Challenger mission rests against the ceiling of the mid-deck to have his breakfast.

or a chair, or a bed. If we fall, we no longer have those sensations. A high diver has a brief experience of weightlessness, and so does someone in a plane that goes into a dive. Gravity is pulling them down, but there is nothing to resist it and create the sensation of weight.

When a spacecraft's engine is firing, the crew members feel themselves being pushed along. They have a sensation of weight. When the engine is turned off, the spacecraft and everything on board are equally affected by gravity. Whether the spacecraft is slowing down, or actually falling back towards Earth, or moving in

circular orbit at constant speed, the raft and its occupants move together. The crew, therefore, have no sensation of weight.

Weightlessness is one of the reasons why a space station could be commercially useful. It might be possible to carry out industrial processes that would be impossible on Earth. It might be possible to make very pure medical drugs, large, perfect crystals for computer microchips and new types of metal. If these plans succeed, space will become even busier than it is already.

▲ Outside the safety of Challenger an astronaut is moved towards the cargo bay by the remote-control arm operated by a colleague inside the spacecraft.

ROBOT

When you hear the word 'robot', you probably think of a walking, talking machine of roughly human appearance, like Artoo-Deetoo and See-Threepio in the film *Star Wars*. One day devices like these may be built and used. But there are already thousands of robots, not looking very much like human beings, at work around the world.

The word 'robot' was invented by a Czech playwright, Karel Čapek, from the word in his language that meant 'work'. Čapek's robots were mechanical men used as factory workers. The word is used loosely for many sorts of automatic machine. But it is best to use it only for machines that perform movements that human beings would otherwise carry out, and that react 'intelligently' to changes in their surroundings. So the mechanical figures that were often built into clocks or fairground organs in past centuries were not robots – they could perform only a fixed set of movements over and over again.

A good example of a robot mechanism is the autopilot. The flight of an airplane can be completely controlled by its autopilot. Information about the aircraft's direction, speed and height, and about its tilt, if any, is constantly sent from the different instruments to a computer. If there is any deviation from the correct values, which have been set by the human pilot, the computer moves the control surfaces on the wings, or changes the engine speed, to make a correction. The autopilot is normally in control for almost the whole flight. The human pilot takes over only for takeoff and landing – and these, too, may soon become fully automatic.

The space probes that travel to distant planets are robot explorers. The mission controllers on Earth cannot control them directly because their radio commands may take hours to travel to the probe. So computers on board the craft must control its manoeuvres near the planet, and its landing. They must do what a human pilot would do if one was on board.

Robots at work

The so-called 'robots' used in factories usually consist of a mechanical arm controlled by a computer. The arm is jointed in one or two places. There is a 'hand' at the end of the arm, which can grip objects. Typical tasks for the robot arm are welding panels to a car body, or painting car bodies, or tightening bolts. Often a single robot can be 'taught' to do any of these tasks. An engineer may program it by typing in instructions, in the same way as a computer is programmed. Or, using tools connected to the robot's computer, the engineer may go through the movements the robot will have to perform. In this way precise information about the movements are transmitted to the robot's computer. Then the robot imitates the movements exactly – but much faster and without ever tiring or making a mistake.

Although they are very versatile, most of these machines cannot react appropriately if something goes slightly wrong. If they are given the wrong component, or the right component in the wrong position, they will go through their usual movements and, say, weld a panel in completely the wrong position. But some industrial robots have simple 'senses' that enable them to detect that something is wrong. They might be equipped with a simple television camera that shows what position a component lying on a conveyor belt is in, so that they can turn their hands into the right position. They might have detectors built into their hands that enable them to adjust the strength of their grip on an object and the force with which they lift it.

Many industrial jobs can be carried out far more quickly and cheaply by robots than by human workers. But we are still a long way from building robots that could carry out all the complicated tasks involved in, say, serving in a department store or doing housework. It will be a long time before we see robot shop assistants or home helps.

▲ Robots are used increasingly where working conditions for humans are unpleasant, for example in car making plants. This robot has a mechanical arm controlled by a computer. The arm's instructions are typed in at the computer's keyboard. The arm is jointed so that the hand can reach things within a distance equal to the arm's length. The hand can swivel at the wrist and the 'fingers' can grip an object.

Robots can now do many different kinds of task, but they still need humans to control them and give them instructions. All the robots in the body shop at this car plant are supervised from this control room.

GLOSSARY

Airplane An aircraft that is propelled by engines and supported by the upward force generated by air flowing over its wings. Its name comes from two Greek words meaning 'wandering through the air'.

Atom The minute particles of which matter is made. Ninety-two types of atom occur naturally on Earth, one for each of the 92 chemical elements. Atoms are made up of three smaller types of particle, called the *proton, neutron* and *electron.*

Cosmic radiation Space is filled with cosmic radiation, which consists of high-energy rays and fast-moving particles. Cosmic radiation is screened off from the ground by the Earth's atmosphere.

Crater A bowl-shaped depression in the ground, formed by either a volcanic explosion or the impact of a *meteor.* Only a few craters survive on Earth, many others having been worn away by wind and rain. Airless worlds, such as the Moon and Mercury, are covered with countless craters.

Density If you take equal volumes of different materials, you will find that they weigh different amounts. Thus a quantity of the liquid metal mercury will weigh 13.6 times as much as an equal volume of water. Mercury is said to have a higher density than water.

Electron One of the fundamental particles that make up the *atom.* Atoms consist of a number of electrons moving in orbits about a central *nucleus.* Electrons can escape from certain atoms, such as those of metals. An electric current consists of moving electrons.

Energy An object is said to have energy when it is possible to obtain useful work from it. Thus steam or a can of petrol or gasoline possess energy, because both can drive engines. Heat, light and electricity are different forms of energy. In fact, matter itself can be transformed into pure energy, as in a nuclear explosion – the matter vanishes, to be replaced by radiation.

Engine A mechanical device that converts energy into force or motion. A car engine uses the energy released when petrol is burned to turn the car wheels. A jet engine uses the energy released by burning fuel to push an aircraft through the air.

Free fall An object that is moving under the influence of *gravity* alone is said to be in 'free fall'. A spacecraft is in free fall when its rocket engine is not firing. Everything in it is then weightless, because everything is moving together – sensations of weight occur only when the pull of gravity is resisted by, for example, the ground.

Friction When two objects are in contact it needs an effort to slide them past each other, no matter how smooth they are. The force that resists motion is called friction. A car is slowed down by the friction of its brakes with the wheels.

Gear Gear wheels have interlocking teeth so that when one turns it makes the wheel in contact with it turn. Gear wheels are used to connect engines with the things they drive – for example, a car engine drives the road wheels through a series of gears. Using gear wheels of different sizes means that the road wheels turn at different rates for a given engine speed.

Gravity/gravitation Every particle of matter attracts every other particle. This force is called gravity. The gravitational attraction of small objects is not noticeable, but the gravitational attraction of a mountain can be measured. And gravitational force is responsible for preventing the oceans, atmosphere and everything else on Earth from escaping into space.

Hydraulics The science of using liquids, such as water or oil, to operate mechanical devices. The word 'hydraulic' is applied to such devices. A car's main brakes, for example, are hydraulic. They are operated by the pressure of the driver's foot on a pedal, transmitted through oil contained in pipes.

Isotope The *atoms* of a chemical element may not all be identical. There may be several different kinds, called isotopes, of that element. The different isotopes behave the same in chemical reactions, but have different numbers of particles in the atomic *nucleus*. For example, one isotope of uranium has 235 particles in its nucleus, while another has 238.

Molecule The smallest amount of a chemical substance that can exist under normal conditions. Sometimes it is just a single *atom*, but often it consists of a cluster of atoms. The carbon dioxide molecule, for example, consists of two oxygen atoms joined to a carbon atom.

Neutron One of the two types of particle that make up the atomic *nucleus*. It is so called because it is electrically neutral – it has no electric charge. Outside the nucleus a neutron survives 16 minutes on average – then it breaks up into an *electron* and a *proton*.

Nucleus The central core of the *atom*. The simplest nucleus is that of the hydrogen atom. It consists of a single *proton*. All other nuclei consist of *neutrons* and protons. *Electrons* revolve around the nucleus. They are very light, and most of the atom's weight is in the nucleus.

Power The rate at which *energy* is delivered by some device.

Pressure The strength of a force divided by the area it is acting on. A heavy suitcase standing on one end causes a certain pressure on the ground. Lying on its side, it creates less pressure. Its weight is the same, but in the second position it is distributed over a larger area. The pressure of the air around us is due to the weight of the atmosphere pressing down on the Earth's surface.

Propellant A material that is used for propelling a projectile, a vehicle or a substance. A rocket may be powered by two propellants: liquid fuel and liquid oxygen, with which the fuel burns. Or the rocket may have a single solid propellant. The gunpowder in a rifle cartridge is a propellant; so is the high-pressure gas that drives a liquid out of a spray can.

Proton One of the two types of particle that make up the atomic *nucleus*. It has a positive electric charge. So the protons in the nucleus repel each other (try to push each other away), because 'like charges repel'. The nucleus would instantly break up but for the *neutrons* that are also present to hold the protons together. In a big nucleus like that of uranium, the repulsion is so strong that the neutrons cannot quite hold the nucleus together, and after a time it splits. Scientists call this splitting fission.

Radioactive/radioactivity A radioactive substance is one in which the *nuclei* of atoms are constantly 'decaying', or breaking down into other types of nucleus. As they do so they send out radiations, consisting of fast-moving particles and high-energy X-rays.

Reaction Every time something exerts a force, there is a reaction – an equal force in the opposite direction. When you fire a rifle, it 'kicks' back against your shoulder. If you pull down on a rope fixed to the ceiling, the reaction will lift you up.

Satellite A body that revolves around a larger one because of its gravitational attraction. The Moon is a satellite of the Earth, and the planets are satellites of the Sun.

Solar system The Sun and all the bodies that revolve around it – the nine major planets, their *satellites*, the asteroids, comets, and interplanetary gas and dust.

Tonne A metric ton or 1000 kilograms. This is equivalent to 2204.6 pounds. It is therefore about 10% larger than the more common short ton of 2,000 pounds.

Vacuum A region that is completely empty of matter. In fact, a true vacuum has never been achieved. The best laboratory vacuum contains traces of gas. In outer space there is a better vacuum – but here, too, there are cosmic rays (sub-atomic particles), gas *molecules* and dust grains.

▼Bob Stewart became the first person to fly freely in space. Here, with his special back pack, he carries out experimental manoeuvres.

INDEX

Airplane
  aileron 7–9
  first flights 7
  guiding 7, 9
  jet engined 9–11,
    40–41
  meaning 6
  supersonic 10
  turbofan 11, 40
  turboprop 40
  wings 6, 8
Aldrin, Edwin (Buzz) 55
Amplifiers 48
Apollo Mission 53
Armstrong, Neil 55
Astronauts 2–3, 52
Atoms 22–23
Autogyros 13
Autopilot 60

B-52 jet bomber 10
Batteries 25, 36
Bernoulli, Jacques 7
Bernoulli's principle 6, 7
Bicycle 33–34
Biplane 7, 8
Boeing 747 jumbo jet 6,
  11
Braking system 34
Breguet, Louis 12
Buoyancy 50–51

Čapek, Karel 60
Car
  engine 35
  petrol engine 31
  phones 26
Cayley, Sir George 6
Challenger mission 58,
  59
Challenger space craft
  20
Columbia 18
Computers 27, 60
Concorde 8, 10, 11, 51
Cornu, Paul 12

Daimler, Gottlieb 30, 31
De Dion tricycle 16
de la Cierva, Juan 13
Diesel, Rudolf 32
Diesel-electric
  locomotive 25, 27
Diesel engine 28, 31–32,
  50, 51

Dynamite 42

Edison phonograph 48
Electric motors 27
Electricity
  atoms 22–23
  cables 23
  current 24
  electrons 22–23
  factories, for 25, 36
  generating 24, 36
  generating plant 23
  generating station 25
  homes, for 25, 36
  information and 27
  resistance 24
  sub-station 23
  voltage 24
Electrons 22–23
Energy conservation
  44–45
Engine
  diesel 28, 31–32, 50,
    51
  four-stroke 30, 31
  internal combustion
    30–31, 32
  jet 9–11, 32, 40–41
  meaning 28
  piston 16–17
  steam 28–29
  two-stroke 31
Explosive 42–43

F-47 Saber 10
F-111 fighter-bomber 7,
  10
Fa-61 helicopter 12–13
Fa-223 helicopter 13
Film, radioactivity
  detected by 47
Fireworks 18, 42
Flywheel 36
Focke, Heinrich 12
Fuel, rocket 18–19

Gagarin, Yuri 52
Gas turbine 40–41
Gears 17, 33, 35
Geiger, Johannes 46
Geiger counter 46–47
General Dynamics
  Corporation 7
Glenn, John 52
Glider 6, 14
Gravitation 52
Gunpowder 42

Hang gliders 14
Hawker Siddeley
  Harrier 9
Heinkel He 178 9
Helicopter
  agility 12
  first 12
  lift 13
  modern 12–13
  passenger-carrying 12
  rotors 13
Hildebrand 16
Holland, John 50
Horse-power 29
Hydrogen bomb 42

Inclined plane 35
Internal combustion
  engine 30–31, 32
Irwin, Jim 55

Jack 33, 35
Japanese sound system
  48
Javelin rocket 19
Jet engine 9–11, 32,
  40–41
Jupiter 56, 57

Kawasaki motorcycle 17
Kinetic energy 45
Kite 6

Lever 34, 35
Lightning 22
Lindbergh, Charles A 8

Machines 33–35
Mechanical arm 60, 61
Microphone
  different types 48
  electrostatic 48
  modern 49
  ribbon 47, 48
  work of amplifiers 48
Moon 55
Motor car see Car
Motorcycle
  first 16
  gears 17
  piston engines 16–17
  racing 16
  shock absorbers 17
  sidecar 17

Nitroglycerine 42
Nobel, Alfred 42
Nobel, Immanuel 42
Nuclear energy 36
Nuclear explosives 42
Nuclear fission 37

Nuclear power station
  36, 38
Nuclear reactor 36–39,
  50
Nutcrackers 33, 35

Orbit 52
Otto, Nikolaus August
  31
Overbalancing wheel 45

Parachute 21
Patents 45
Perpetual motion 44–45
Pliers 33
Plutonium 38
Pulley 34, 35

Radio phones 26
Radioactivity 46–47
Remote Maintenance
  Vehicle 51
Robot 56, 60–61
Rocket 29
Rocket
  fuel 18–19
  launch 52
  principles behind 18
  retro 52
  Saturn V 19–20
Rutherford, Ernest 46

Sailplanes 14
Salyut stations 56
Satellites
  communications 53–54
  unmanned 52–53
  uses 53
Saturn 56, 57
Saturn V rocket 19–20
Screw 35
Skylab 52, 56, 58
Sikorsky, Igor 13
Snorkel 51
Snow scooter 17
Sobrero, Ascanio 42
Sonic booms 10
Sopwith Pup fighter 8
Space exploration 54–56
Space flight 52–59
Space probes 56, 60
Space rockets 19–20
Space stations 56, 59
Spanner 35
Spirit of St Louis 8
Spitfire fighters 8
Sputnik 52
Steam engines 28–29
Stephenson, George 29
Stuart, Herbert Akroyd
  32
Submarine 50–51
Submersibles 51
Sugar tongs 33
Supersonic flight 10

TNT 42
Telephones 26, 27,
  47–48
Thermals 14
Trinitrotoluene 42
Triton 50
Turbines 40–41

Uranium 36–38

Venus 56
Viking missions 56
Voyager probes 56, 57

Water mill 44–45
Water turbine 41
Watt, James 28
Weightlessness 56,
  58–59
Werner, Eugene 16
Werner, Michael 16
Wheel overbalancing
Windlass 33
Windmill 40
Wolfmuller 16
Wrench 35
Wright, Orville 6, 7,
Wright, Wilbur 6, 7,

Acknowledgments

ATP, Boeing, Bonetti/
Terreni, British
Aerospace, British
Telecom, Daily
Telegraph Colour
Library, Jacques
Dubourg, Fiat, Flight
Picture Library,
Hawker-Siddeley,
Headway Public
Relations, David Higgs
Michael Holford,
Hoverspeed UK,
Archivio IGDA, The
Image Bank, Imperial
War Museum, Keyston
Press Agency, Mansell
Collection, Don Morley
NASA, Nat's Photo,
Photri, Picturepoint, R
6 Melodium, A Rizzi, C
Roberts, Science Photo
Library, Shell
Photographic Library,
Spectrum Colour
Library, Frank Spoone
Pictures, F Tomasi, US
Army, United Kingdom
Atomic Energy
Commission, Vauxhall
Motors, Graham
Wiltshire, ZEFA.